The Walnut Tree

The Walnut Tree

Geoffrey Ursell
Based on the Novel by Martha Blum

The Walnut Tree
first published 2012 by
Scirocco Drama
An imprint of J. Gordon Shillingford Publishing Inc.
© 2012 Geoffrey Ursell
Adapted from the novel by Martha Blum

Scirocco Drama Editor: Glenda MacFarlane
Cover design by Terry Gallagher/Doowah Design Inc.
Printed and bound in Canada on 100% post-consumer recycled paper.

We acknowledge the financial support of the Manitoba Arts Council and The Canada Council for the Arts for our publishing program.

All rights reserved. No part of this book may be reproduced, for any reason, by any means, without the permission of the publisher. This play is fully protected under the copyright laws of Canada and all other countries of the Copyright Union and is subject to royalty. Changes to the text are expressly forbidden without written consent of the author. Rights to produce, film, record in whole or in part, in any medium or in any language, by any group amateur or professional, are retained by the author.
Production inquiries should be addressed to:
Geoffrey Ursell
ursell@sasktel.net

Library and Archives Canada Cataloguing in Publication

Blum, Martha, 1913-2007
  The walnut tree / Martha Blum, Geoffrey Ursell

A play.
ISBN 978-1-897289-74-7

    I. Title.

PS8553.L858W34 2012   C812'.54   C2012-901282-3

J. Gordon Shillingford Publishing
P.O. Box 86, RPO Corydon Avenue, Winnipeg, MB Canada R3M 3S3

In loving memory of
Martha Blum (1913-2007)
and
Irene Blum (1948-2009)

Acknowledgments

My sincere thanks to everyone involved in the development and production of this play. They include Brian Mallard, Tibor Feheregyhazi, Del Surjik, Sheldon Born, Angus Ferguson, Irene Blum, Will Brooks, Louisa Ferguson, Johnna Wright, Deborah Buck, the workshop actors, and all the cast and crew. And thanks, most of all, to my dear friend Martha Blum for providing me with such a compelling and beautiful novel to adapt to the stage.

The play is based on the book published by Coteau Books, and was commissioned, developed, and premiered by Persephone Theatre.

Set

Act I begins in the bedroom of Süssel's 1997 Saskatoon home, (on one side of the stage) suggested by two walls. There's a modern bed with a walnut headboard and footboard, and three drawers beneath it. Above the bed hangs a smallish carpet, "no bigger than a good-sized mirror." It has a "Tree of Life" pattern, depicting a shiny blue tree with its roots in other trees, each treetop interweaving with the roots of the tree beyond. Strange birds sit on the tree branches. Silky, shiny, with birds of silver, gold, copper, a mysterious world, framed in the pattern of a carpet." Süssel's bathrobe lies on the bottom of the bed, her slippers beside the bed.

As the play proceeds, Süssel's home in Czernowitz is indicated by two moveable "trucks" carrying suitcases and trunks formed into ranks that can be climbed on. These trucks are positioned in varying places to indicate other rooms and locations, including a cattle car. Old wooden chairs and suitcases form the other elements of the set.

The Musician sits at a grand piano, which can be moved around the stage as required.

Time and Place

Act I: ....Saskatoon in 1997 and Czernowitz and area from 1921 to 1943.

Act II: ....Saskatoon, Czernowitz, Bucharest, and Israel from 1944 to 1966.

Characters

(6 Women—one a Musician, and 4 Men)

Süssel

Young Süssel (from age 15 to 45), also ensemble

Max (from age 15 to 45), also ensemble

Ileana, also Ludmilla Bunin and ensemble

Marusja, also Helen and ensemble

Süssel's Mother and ensemble

Süssel's Father, also Waiter and ensemble

Felix, also Sergei, also Dmitry,
also Young Nazi, also Joey, also Grisha

German Lover, also Dr. Hermann Bauer,
also Soviet Army Officer,
also Romanian Policeman and ensemble

Production History

The Walnut Tree had its premiere production at Persephone Theatre, Saskatoon, Saskatchewan, from September 23 to October 7, 2009, with the following cast and crew:

Robert Benz..Süssel's Father and ensemble

Deborah Buck..Musician

Matthew Burgess...Max and ensemble

Devon Dubnyk..Felix, Grisha and ensemble

Louise Ferguson...................................Süssel's Mother and ensemble

Kristina Hughes..................................Marusja, Helen and ensemble

Jamie Lee Shebelski...Young Süssel

Marie Stillin..Süssel

Kevin Williamson..Dr. Bauer and ensemble

Johnna Wright.....................................Ileana, Ludmilla and ensemble

Directed by Angus Ferguson

Assistant Director: Will Brooks

Set Design by Carla Orosz

Costume Design by Evgenia Mikhaylova

Design Dramaturge / Production Design & Lighting Design by Del Surjik

Assistant Lighting Designer: Byron Hnatuk

Movement Coach: Natasha Martina

Stage Manager: Laura Kennedy

Assistant Stage Manager: Diana Domm

Apprentice Stage Manager: Jennifer Rathie-Wright

Music was selected by Deborah Buck in consultation with Martha Blum and Geoffrey Ursell, or created and arranged by Deborah Buck. All original music copyright Deborah Buck, and SOCAN.

Geoffrey Ursell

Geoffrey Ursell is an award-winning writer of drama for stage, television, and radio, as well as of fiction, poetry, and songs. His stage plays have won three national playwriting awards, and his novel *Perdue* won the Books in Canada First Novel Award. His musical comedy *Saskatoon Pie!* has been produced twice and toured provincially by Persephone Theatre. Other plays include *Winning the Prairie Gamble* (a collaboration with Barbara Sapergia) for Persephone's SaskTel Youth Tour Centennial Year, and *Gold on Ice* (a musical celebration of the Sandra Schmirler curling team) at Dancing Sky Theatre. His dramatization of Martha Blum's novel *The Walnut Tree* opened Persephone's 2009/2010 season, and his thriller *Dead Midnight* opened the theatre's 2011/2012 season. Geoffrey is also a founding member and current President of the nationally esteemed publisher Coteau Books. He was awarded the Saskatchewan Order of Merit in 2009 for his work in the arts.

Martha Blum

Martha Blum was born in 1913 in Czernowitz, Austria. She immigrated to Canada in 1951 by way of Israel, and moved to Saskatoon in 1954, working as a pharmacist and teaching musical interpretation. Her novel *The Walnut Tree* won two Saskatchewan Book Awards and was nominated for the Canadian Booksellers Association's Ex Libris Award. She also published a short story collection, *Children of Paper*, and another novel, *The Apothocary*, a sequel to *The Walnut Tree*. In the fall of 1998, Martha was one of 50 Holocaust survivors—both Jewish and non-Jewish—who received national citations from the Human Rights Commission for their contributions to Canadian society: hers was in the area of the arts. Martha died in 2007.

Act I

Scene One: Dreaming, Süssel's bedroom in her Saskatoon home, 1997

Sound of sleeping breathing, clock ticking. The MUSICIAN begins to play fragments of "Träumerei" ("Dreaming") from Robert Schumman's "Kinderszenen."

Dim light up on SÜSSEL, who lies in bed, sleeping.

Voices softly, but urgently, begin to call SÜSSEL's name.

VOICES: Süssel. Süssel. Sweetie! Süssel!

As they call, lights come up on several figures in the background. They are her MOTHER, her red hair piled up high in a chignon, wearing a blue and black silk dress. Her FATHER, his hair the colour of ebony, impeccably dressed in a suit. Her older brother, FELIX, in a yellow shirt and maroon suit. MARUSJA, their Ukrainian servant. DR. HERMAN BAUER, in a Nazi officer's uniform. And MAX.

SÜSSEL stirs as they call, but does not wake. They speak to her more urgently.

MOTHER: Some things have to be said.

FATHER: This is where the future lies.

FELIX:	Dance with me. Dance.
BAUER:	I did not make that war.
MARUSJA:	What would you know, a young spoilt rich girl?
ILEANA:	The Voice has spoken.
MAX:	I will go there for you. I will.
ALL:	Some things have to be said. Some things have to be said. Some things have to be said!

All but MAX move back into the darkness as they speak this line.

MAX: Listen to me, Süssel, listen! There may not be much time.

MAX leaves. Lights down on all but SÜSSEL.

SÜSSEL: *(In her sleep.)* Max! Don't go! Max!

MANOLE'S WIFE screams. Music stops with the scream. SÜSSEL wakes with a start.

Again...again. Night after night I am wakened by that last scream. Why? But there was...there was something more in my dreams. Yes. My father, mother, brother, and Marusja and Doctor Bauer, I saw them all. And Max. Dear Max. What did he say? What does he want me to do? "Some things have to be said." All right. I'll try to say them. Maybe then they'll leave me in peace.

Opens drawers of the bed and rummages in them.

Where is something when you need it? Aha!

Pulls out pad of paper and pen. Closes drawer. Props up pillows. She is poised to write.

All right. I'll start. I'll start. Then maybe the past will stay in the past. But I've never written down a story before. So where to begin? *(Pause. Thinks.)*

"Horn Dance" from "Romanian Folk Dances" by Bela Bartok begins, and it's as if SÜSSEL is aware of it, but only subconsciously.

The music goes under the MASTER MANOLE story.

Ah, yes. Ileana. Our Romanian housemaid Ileana, who looked after me. I haven't thought of her for at least fifty years. Why start with her? Ah, well, why not? All right, with Ileana. And, oh, that story she told me.

Scene Two: Master Manole, the Geller family home in Czernowitz, 1921

ILEANA appears on the other side of the stage. She carries a chair in, sets it down, and sits on it as she speaks. ILEANA wears a skirt with a brâu (a wide loomed belt with stripes in all colours) around its waist, and an embroidered blouse.

ILEANA: Come, Jewish child, come sit with me. Night is falling, a dusk as long and as beautiful as my story.

SÜSSEL: *(Begins to write as she speaks.)* A story. Promised to me for good behaviour. A promise coming true; as stillness settles. I always long for this hour, when Ileana's work is done and it is in-between times. Not yet dark, but there is shimmery silence.

SÜSSEL gets out of bed, puts down the pen and paper.

Oh, it is totally ours, this moment. Ileana and I know that Father and Mother have gone down to the wine cellar for the evening glass of wine, for the cigarette taken from a silver case, burnt hazelnuts, a chat with neighbours. Who cares about my big, fat brother, Felix? It is all ours, time, the kitchen bench, and the stove still glowing with slowly dying coals.

Dusk, our time for stories. *(Music ends.)* And Ileana's lap, where a five-year-old would find her sweetest home.

SÜSSEL goes to ILEANA and lies down with her head on ILEANA's lap.

ILEANA: Yes, this story is the most holy legend of the Romanian people. It is about Master Manole. He is a master builder, a mason. But he is also a great holy man, a man of God.

One night, Manole hears the Voice! Master, build Me a house of prayer, contemplation, and learning, God says. A home of glory. Manole, awe-struck, trembling, falls to his knees, makes the sign of the cross. *(She shows SÜSSEL how to make the sign of the cross.)* He understands. God has found him worthy among all His Romanian children to build a cathedral to His glory. Near the Curtea de Arges, one of the oldest cities in Romania, on the Arges River.

He goes to work. Assembles all he needs, utensils, wood, stone. The villagers help. They revere Manole, for God has chosen him. The work goes well, the foundations are laid, and he sleeps soundly.

But somewhere, sometime, things begin to go wrong, and whatever he has built in the daytime crumbles in the night. He picks up his stones in the morning, puts one on top of the other with much more care. But lo and behold, the next day he finds all he has built with so much love and vision broken on the ground.

Master Manole prays and prays. He can neither eat nor sleep. And then, one day, when he is deep in thought, the answer comes. He hears the unmistakable Voice. Take what you love best and offer it to Me. Take it to the cathedral and wall in what you love. Then the house of God will be built. Then I will know my true servant.

SÜSSEL
& ILEANA: The Voice has spoken.

MOTHER enters unseen and listens.

ILEANA: So Manole takes his beautiful wife, puts her into the side chapel, and starts to set stone on stone.

As ILEANA speaks, SÜSSEL is becoming disturbed.

And before the last stone is set, he hears her scream for air. *(Both ILEANA and MANOLE'S WIFE scream.)* So he sets the stone fast, fast, so as not to weaken in his service to God.

And now the Curtea de Arges cathedral stands in its glory forever and—

SÜSSEL moves from ILEANA's lap to the floor, on her knees, shouting, like a child.

SÜSSEL: Let her out! Let her out, Ileana! I don't want her in there, she has no air, she can't breathe! I don't care about your terrible cathedral, let her out, Ileana. Let her out, let her out! *(She starts sobbing.)*

ILEANA: You stupid Jewish child, you understand nothing holy. I'm wasting my time. There is no way a Christian can be made out of a Jew.

MOTHER: *(Steps forward.)* That's enough, Ileana. Go and bring some firewood in.

ILEANA: There's plenty of—

MOTHER: Go!

Scene Three: My Question

>ILEANA *exits.* MOTHER *sits down in the chair and comforts* SÜSSEL, *who stays on the floor.* MOTHER *puts her arms around* SÜSSEL's *head and strokes her face.* SÜSSEL's *sobs ease and cease during the following.*
>
>MUSICIAN *begins softly to play a single line of notes from* "Wiegenlied," *a lullaby by Mozart, under* MOTHER's *speech.*

MOTHER: Hush, hush, my sweet. Hush. Nothing could ever happen to that lovely Lady Manole. God is good, Süssel. You are a Jewish child. Remember the story of Abraham. He also heard the Voice of God and was to bring his son Isaac as a sacrifice, and at the last moment, as Abraham's arm was raised to slay his son, God held his arm and spoke: It is enough, you have shown that you are my faithful servant! So you see, my sweet, Lady Manole surely must have slipped away. Hush, hush.

>*Piano accompaniment as* MOTHER *begins to sing. After a moment,* SÜSSEL *leaves her embrace and slowly moves away from her, as if letting this memory go.*

Schlafe, mein Süssel, schlaf ein
es ruhn Schäfchen und Vögelein
Garten und Wiese verstummt,
auch nicht ein Bienchen mehr summt.
Luna mit silbernem Schein
Gucket zum Fenster herein;
schlafe beim silbernen
Schein!
Schlafe, mein Prinzchen, schlaf ein!

>*Moves away, taking the chair.*

Schlaf ein, schlaf ein!

During this, SÜSSEL returns to her bed, picks up paper and pen. Music fades.

SÜSSEL: *(Angry.)* Here is my question to you, dearest Jehoshua: Why did the stones that Master Manole laid in the daytime crumble at night? And how did the screams of the lovely lady strengthen the stone to stand firm until the cathedral was built? I may have been just a stupid Jewish five-year-old, as Ileana says, but I will never enter your house! *(Writes.)* That scream holds the wall up. It is her soul that is the mortar. *(Stops writing.)* I want none of it. But it's with me as I sleep and… Please explain it to me, because I still don't understand. *(She settles back in bed.)* Am I done? Is that the end?

MUSICIAN plays melody of "Florian Geyer."

No! No, no, no! What am I thinking? How can I forget Max? *(She begins to write furiously.)* Of course! Max. That's where I should have started in the first place. Not with Ileana. No. When is the first time I really see him? Ah, yes. He's hiding across from our home—an apartment on the third floor of my grandfather's house—watching for me to come out. *(She laughs.)* He's…what? Yes, fifteen years old. Leaving childhood behind. His feet are too big, his belt too loose.

Scene Four: Max

A gangly MAX appears.

SÜSSEL: And where am I? Ah, there! Also fifteen.

The young SÜSSEL runs on. She has red hair, knit and knotted like yarn, falling from the crown to the shoulders half into her face, barely revealing the green of her eyes. She has on heavy hiking boots.

And that's what I really look like! Like a wild

thing. *(Laughs.)* Ready to hike off up the mountain. Anyway, I've seen Max for days, standing there under the eavestrough overhang.

YOUNG S: What's your name, stranger? Are you a statue made of stone, or do you have blood in your veins?

She laughs mockingly.

MAX: Max. I'm Max.

SÜSSEL and YOUNG SÜSSEL both laugh. MAX starts to leave. She calls after him.

YOUNG S: Come along, then.

MAX whistles an ancient tune of the German peasant wars, Florian Geyer leading the mob. YOUNG S whistles back in harmony. She takes his hand. They run off, whistling as SÜSSEL speaks. A rollicking version of the music continues under:

SÜSSEL: Whistling a song of rebellion. Leaving Czernowitz behind, then always a different path up Cecina. Cecina, holy as all mountains are holy, wooded to the top, water springing from every crevice. Trolls, elves, and lovers lurk in dark branches, and clearings suddenly appear before you with a sun as loud and yellow as a trumpet.

YOUNG S comes back on. Music stops.

SÜSSEL & YOUNG S: Cecina!

MAX comes back on.

SÜSSEL: I remember…yes, I remember a strenuous climb deep in the Carpathian mountains. We find a cool stalagmite cave. And as we rest… *(She begins to write again.)*

YOUNG S: Max, I want to go to the Dead Sea caves. God speaks to the prophets there. I want His voice. It's written on parchment or held by the ancient stone and released to those who yearn for it. I'm sure there's something we need to learn there. Something that tells us we are one tree. Something portentous will come out of that desert. It's waiting there. Some rescue that will come from the dry sands, the emaciated seer. Perhaps lost texts reside there as eons pass.

MAX: Lost texts?

YOUNG S: About Jews and Christians. And if I can't go, you must.

MAX: I must?

YOUNG S: Absolutely. Do you understand, Max?

MAX: *(Laughing at her.)* Absolutely.

SÜSSEL: Another day, I remember it so very well, we go down to the river. *(Pause.)* I wonder why I spend so much time with Max. I'm not in love with him.

> *SÜSSEL spreads a blanket for them and sits back on the bed, watching. YOUNG S lies down on the blanket and MAX sits beside her, drawing with a pencil.*

MAX: Look how simple truth can be, a shape like a triangle, a circle, a rhomb. Without magic. The truth is here. I will show it to you, Süssel, without incantations or the priestly swinging of myrrh. Just beauty in itself, *(Gazes at her.)* forever... Unless modified and changed by the moving times. Do you know Johannes Kepler's three theorems of orbital motion?

YOUNG S: Three theorems of what?

MAX: Orbital motion.

SÜSSEL: As if I want to hear about Kepler. Foolish boy. Is this how you should talk to me if you want me to love you?

MAX: First, that the planets move in ellipses. Second—

YOUNG S: *(She leaps up.)* Let's go swimming.

MAX: But the river is almost over its banks.

YOUNG S: Let's swim below the bridge.

MAX: No, no, I don't know how well you swim. It'd be too dangerous, especially past the bridge.

YOUNG S: Come, Max. Come!

> *She flings off her sweater and dashes off. He gathers up the blanket and sweater and runs after her.*

MAX: Wait for me! Wait for me! *(Exits.)*

SÜSSEL: Of course I almost drown. But he saves my life, so I promise to marry him. *(Laughs.)* Which doesn't mean I want him trailing around after me all the time.

> *YOUNG S returns. MAX follows her from a distance. She stops and confronts him.*

YOUNG S: Max, I've seen you. *(He stops.)* Don't follow me. No one will conquer me. It is I who conquer, who chooses. I've promised to marry you, fine. And it's true, no one could love me with such perseverance. I love your joy to know, it's all over your face. And above all, I know you'll always be here for me.

> *MAX looks heartened.*

But I have wild ways. I'm my own master and I won't be possessed by anyone. Yes, I've promised to marry you, but I just might not. Max, I can only give you what I can, the rest is mine alone. Stop following me, or you'll be hurt.

She runs off. MAX, sick at heart, turns and goes off the other way.

SÜSSEL: He keeps following me anyway. And we are always running up Cecina, lying in fields, eating picnics at the river. Somehow, I keep finding myself in his company. Why does that keep happening? *(Lost in thought for a moment.)*

MUSICIAN plays café music, "Estrellita" by M.A. Ponce, underscoring the scene. YOUNG S returns. MAX awaits her.

Ah, then one day, one day I say—

YOUNG S: Let's just be civilized and go to a café. We've never done that.

They sit at a small table in the Kucharczyk café. A WAITER brings them Krapfen—a chocolate-covered sweet bread, and hot chocolate with cream. MAX cannot eat or drink. OTHERS sit in the background at another table.

Come, the world hasn't ended. I can see you're on your famous tragic bent—eyes watery, hands sweaty—not saying much. You live your life in hiding.

MAX: It's a different kind of life—that's all.

YOUNG S: But I don't live that way. Oh Max, do eat your Krapfen, it's extraordinary today.

MAX: You'll wait for me, Süssel, you will. *(He takes her hand and with a pencil draws a circle around her ring finger.)* There. To remind you of me. To remind you we're engaged.

YOUNG S: Yes, I know I promised. When I was fifteen it was nice to think I had a fiancé. And you'd just pulled me out of the river. But Max, it was kid's stuff. I'm sixteen now. I'm too wild for you, Max. I have to find love on my own terms. Love just given to me will never be enough.

She takes his hand, holds it. Their knees touch.

Max, do you remember me talking about the Dead Sea caves?

MAX: Yes.

YOUNG S: Well, I've thought about it. When you're grown up, you should go.

MAX: Me? Why me?

YOUNG S: You have a Jewish father and a Lutheran mother. You are both Jew and Christian. A perfect combination.

MAX: Really?

YOUNG S: You'll learn more than I could.

MAX: You're the one who's so keen. Why don't you go?

YOUNG S: I know it's meant to be you. I don't know if I'll ever go there, but you, my sweet friend, you will. For me.

She squeezes his hands.

MAX: Süssel...I will go there for you...I will. *(Music stops.)*

SÜSSEL: Now I know what I was asking. If only I'd known it then. Some things need not have happened. Ah, well, what it is to be so young. Anyway, enough about Max for the moment. What's next?

MUSICIAN plays "Liebeslied" by Fritz Kreisler, underscoring the dance scene.

Scene Five: The Dance

SÜSSEL: *(Delighted.)* Dancing! Dancing!

> *The walls of SÜSSEL's room dance away as FELIX enters. He is a svelte, slender-in-shoulder-and-hip young Apollo. Hair a golden-brown wave lying loose around his ears and neck—daring for the time...a chiselled jaw and a magnificent head set haughtily on his shoulders. He wears a vivid citron-yellow shirt and a maroon suit. The trucks are positioned to indicate the walls of the apartment in Czernowitz.*

Dancing with my brother, Felix. He's so handsome and beauteous: Hübsch und Schön. He's gorgeous. *(She laughs.)* The girls go wild.

> *YOUNG S enters. She now wears a dress in the style of the "new wave of crêpe georgette, dresses in kerchiefs, triangles, like fairy-fringes hanging, the belt at the hip...hair long, hennaed, curled up on top—the equal of my mother's. My muslin dress both concealed and revealed, falling from the open neck past the knee. Beige. The new beige, sometimes a hint of grey in it, the famous greyge."*

But he's mine. And I hold on to him with a ferocity I never show later with any lover. But this is different: I am his also.

FELIX: Dance with me. Dance!

> *FELIX and YOUNG S dance, while SÜSSEL gets up and moves in her own way to the music.*

SÜSSEL: Such wonderful music! There was always music when I was with Felix.

> *As FELIX and YOUNG S dance, they speak.*

YOUNG S: Let's not marry anyone!

FELIX:	We'll have lovers on the side.
YOUNG S:	We'll pool our inheritance, make a mansion.
FELIX:	First we'll have a ballroom the size of Versailles!
YOUNG S:	With mirrors, light from all sides doubling and quadrupling in their silvery surfaces.
FELIX:	A glass dome to reveal the sky above.
YOUNG S:	Parquet laid in diagonal stripes of old oak, shiny honey.
SÜSSEL:	*(Dancing.)* Ha! What fun! What fun!

FELIX and YOUNG S dance on during SÜSSEL's speech.

Spinning strings of interweaving dreams threaded with childhood's chosen pearls. Such fun! The spirit of the thirties: a sensuous lightness of heart, Versailles-castles in the air...and dance floors.

ILEANA enters. FELIX breaks away from YOUNG S to dance with her, in a sexual way.

Oh, and then Mother catches Felix with Ileana in the attic.

MOTHER enters in an elegant black dress. MOTHER points to ILEANA to leave, which she reluctantly does. FELIX, shame-faced, goes off, shrugging to YOUNG S. FATHER enters and he dances first with YOUNG S, then with MOTHER. FATHER leaves. Dance music stops. YOUNG S picks up a book to read.

From offstage comes the sound of screams. DMITRY is beating MARUSJA.

What's that noise now? Those shouts? Those blows? Ah, yes.

YOUNG S: *(To MOTHER.)* He's beating her again!

MOTHER: *(To SÜSSEL.)* Don't interfere with the servants.

YOUNG S: *(Furious.)* I'll kill Dmitry. I'll kill him. He's a loudmouth brute!

MOTHER: He's been drinking. Marusja will be fine.

YOUNG S: I'm going to stop him!

SÜSSEL: Our new housemaid and her husband.

> *She stomps out. The screams have stopped before YOUNG S can have got there. After a moment, YOUNG S returns with MARUSJA, in Ukrainian dress and an apron.*

MARUSJA: *(To MOTHER.)* He loves me. This is how he shows it, I wouldn't know otherwise.

YOUNG S: *(To MOTHER.)* He was already passed out when I got there. Snoring!

MARUSJA: *(To YOUNG S.)* He loves me. *(Indicates her injured face.)* Look, Süssel, how he loves me. But what would you know, a young spoilt rich girl.

YOUNG S: I'm not spoiled!

MOTHER & SÜSSEL: Yes, you are.

> *MARUSJA and MOTHER leave. MUSICIAN begins to play "Der Nussbaum" ("The Walnut Tree") by Schumann.*

SÜSSEL: Yet on we dance. And we sing.

FELIX & YOUNG S: *(Enter and start to sing.)* "Es grünet ein Nußbaum vor dem Haus."

SÜSSEL: Schumann's *"The Walnut Tree."* Such music. Such memories. Unforgettable.

FELIX &
YOUNG S: Duftig, luftig
             Breitet er blättrig die Blätter aus

             FELIX exits. Music continues.

SÜSSEL: What are the last lines? A girl—ah, yes—the blossoms whisper to a girl about a bridegroom. Leaves rustle in the tree as she sinks, smiling, filled with longing and imagining, into sleep and dreams.

             "Longing and imagining." I'm full of that when I am seventeen.

             Music ends.

             And ready to act on it, too.

Scene Six: The German lover

             YOUNG S moves as if to look in a mirror, that is, facing the audience, and takes off one dress and puts on another, tailor-made Herrenfaçon in navy blue, with a Herrenhut, white with a brown band.

SÜSSEL: In the huge mirror of the armoire—carved walnut, Venetian glass—I see myself at seventeen, as if for the first time. A different body faces me, a stranger of such beauty it stops my heartbeat, my breath. Someone else's body and soul. And it shows its fury. It demands silk stockings and patent-leather pumps. It demands and receives.

YOUNG S: *(Finished changing, she moves to put away the old dress and pick up books.)* What do I need with the old, the familiar, the conformist? What do I need with do's and don't's, with eyes spying, with rabbis and their courts? Another road of glory lies before me, stretched like a silver band. No need for shelter, tribe, or fold! *(Lifts up a book to see what it is.)* Greek.

(*Shouts.*) Dead, dead, dead! (*Flings it away. Then another book.*) Latin. (*Shouts. Flings the book.*) It's dead, all dead! The world is mine! Mine!

MUSICIAN *plays Andante portion of "Sinfonia" from J.S. Bach's Second Partita as piano is moved to downstage left. Trucks are moved upstage.*

The GERMAN LOVER, *"fortyish and balding, Germanic looking" enters, humming or vocalizing to the music, his hands moving as if he's conducting. (Later, he becomes conductor of Czernowitz's small orchestra, the Collegium Musicum).*

SÜSSEL: From the Heights of the Hapsburgs Gardens you can look out over the city to where Cecina blocks the river's path, forcing it to make a bend around its cliffs. A sharp precipice and a wide look across the river valley, where I come to rest.

YOUNG S *enters and sees him. He carries on conducting Bach.*

LOVER: I lost my wife to mental despair. A beautiful thing she had been. I lived with her for ten years. She ate oranges with peel, without feeling the sting of volatile oils in the skin. One day she went into the attic, put herself into a trunk, and closed the lid. (*Beat.*) Do you know the music of Johann Sebastian Bach?

YOUNG S: No.

LOVER: He is my church now. In him the glory of the opposing, counterpoint, joining sounds in harmony A tongue, a world. Speaking through itself directly to the heart with no one in between, no rabbi, no priest. What is your name?

YOUNG S: Süssel.

LOVER: Süssel. Come with me, my sweet Jewish child. I'll play for you.

MUSICIAN plays as they cross the stage to take over SÜSSEL's bed. They begin to undress. As they do so, SÜSSEL puts on her bathrobe and, taking her pen and paper, moves away from the bed.

YOUNG S: Fat Frumos din Lacrima.

LOVER: What is that?

YOUNG S: The Romanian Prince Charming. The beautiful lad born from a tear. As you are born from a tear, my prince.

Lights down on LOVER and YOUNG S. getting into bed.

SÜSSEL: "Do not worry. It won't hurt," my German lover says.

YOUNG S cries out once in pain. Bach's music stops.

But it does. And I know now that all of us are born from a tear. *(Beat.)* I give myself to him with such savage abandon as if to God. It's new to him. He has to both learn and teach. Days and days of taking and giving our bodies. In search of the skill to unlock the unknown.

LOVER: We reach God the way we reach Him, by the myriad ways of the imagination. Everything will do.

He starts to stroke her like the Mexican boy strokes the Pietà.

I once stood in front of a young Mexican boy viewing a Pietà. Christ across his mother's lap, the head reclining, the left arm dangling elegantly, as if alive. He stood for a long time, then slowly approached the body and touched the tips of Christ's fingers, stroking the hand finger by finger, the palm, the wrist, up the forearm and upper arm, and then returned to touch his own fingers,

	the palm of his hand, and so on, touching all of Christ's fallen body and his own, a deliberate, slow stroking. It took all morning. I walked out of the Church de la Guadeloupe in a trance. I had seen God. Sweetie, come, you're clever. Look at the Lord in Johann Sebastian.
SÜSSEL:	Of course I can read music, but the heaven of Johann Sebastian I learn from my handsome "lad born out of a tear." *(Music ends.)*

Scene Seven: The Musician

SÜSSEL:	What was that piece he played? Something from "The Well-Tempered Clavier"?
	Light up on MUSICIAN.
MUSICIAN:	It was the Second Partita actually.
SÜSSEL:	Ah, that's right. It was— *(Amazed.)* Who are you? I'm not remembering you. You're not one of—
MUSICIAN:	—the others? No. Do you think you could do all this without music?
SÜSSEL:	Do all what?
MUSICIAN:	This. Remembering.
SÜSSEL:	I hadn't thought about it.
MUSICIAN:	Precisely. Music has always been part of your life.
SÜSSEL:	Of course. I can't imagine my life without music.
MUSICIAN:	Exactly.
SÜSSEL:	Ah, I see.
MUSICIAN:	Well, then, shall we continue?
SÜSSEL:	*(Laughs.)* Yes. And you'll help me?

MUSICIAN: Yes, I will.

SÜSSEL: Well, then, where was I?

> *MUSICIAN plays a phrase of Bach.*

Ah, that's it. My German lover.

> *MUSICIAN nods and plays a cabaret piece, while the trucks are put back in position for the apartment.*

Lege artis, the real Berlin. This is what he means to me at seventeen. Berlin: the great German world, of freedom, letters, boulevards, young witty sharp tongues, frivolity, and the street eroticism of cabaret. *(Beat.)* Then I see him with someone else. It cuts deep. But I decide to get on with life. I pass my entrance exam to the university, the top student in science and languages. I expect praise.

Scene Eight: Father and choosing

> *YOUNG S stands looking in a mirror, examining her looks. MARUSJA brings in a soup tureen and sets it down. MOTHER is hanging on the wall a small carpet, of trees whose branches intertwine with the roots of the tree above, a "Tree of Life" carpet with silver birds sitting in its branches. MARUSJA leaves.*

MOTHER: *(Looks at carpet.)* There. How beautiful it is. Thank you, Marusja. Süssel, my child, come let me hug you; I want to hold you for a moment, I so long for it!

> *YOUNG S does not move.*

Please, Süssel.

> *YOUNG S moves to MOTHER and permits her hands to be held.*

Heavens, how grown up you look.

Impatiently, YOUNG S pulls away from MOTHER as FATHER enters.

FATHER: Come, Süssel, into the salon. We'll talk.

YOUNG S continues to admire herself in the mirror.

SÜSSEL: I hate that tone.

MOTHER: Go, Sweetheart, it's just a friendly talk, to congratulate you on passing your baccalaureate with such high marks.

YOUNG S follows FATHER into the salon. He offers her a chair, which she refuses.

SÜSSEL: I know better.

MOTHER: The soup will stay hot.

YOUNG S and FATHER turn to face each other.

FATHER: Süssel, I expect you to make a pharmacy degree first and then go into post-graduate work in biochemistry.

SÜSSEL moves into this scene, circling around the others, observing FATHER.

YOUNG S: I know what you want.

SÜSSEL: You should at least ask me what I want.

FATHER: Wonderful things are happening: both you and Felix live in the most exciting scientific times. This is where the future lies.

SÜSSEL: I know, and Felix knows, we're being groomed for succession.

FATHER: Süssel, I need you and Felix by me to continue my work and take it over.

SÜSSEL: Here I am being treated as a child.

FATHER: Of course, the choice of universities is yours. Felix, as you know, chose Vienna.

SÜSSEL: My cheeks burn with anger.

YOUNG S: *(Confronting him.)* Father, you haven't asked me what I want to do.

FATHER: *(He sits down.)* Yes, Süssel, what is it you want to do…other than pharmacy?

SÜSSEL: Your face looks pained and drawn, worried. How much or what do you know about me? I wonder. I have lain with my lover. Do you know? My passionate ways are yours. So you must.

YOUNG S: In truth, I don't want to do anything else. Pharmacy interests me. But I do want to study Slavic languages on the side and this is why I'll choose Prague first. Then I'll go for French, to Strasbourg.

SÜSSEL: I kiss you fast on both cheeks before I cry.

YOUNG S kisses him on both cheeks.

FATHER: That's settled then. Good luck, Süssel my daughter.

SÜSSEL moves away. Lights down on all others. MUSICIAN plays Dvorak under the following. Trucks change position. YOUNG S brings on two chairs during the following.

Scene Nine: Prague and Impreccor

SÜSSEL: How do I spend the next few years? Learning, of course. Languages and sciences. I fall in love with youth itself, with the grey morning stone city.

YOUNG S: *(Arms flung wide to embrace the city.)* Prague!

SÜSSEL: Smetana and Dvorak in the streets everywhere. I tremble with memory.

YOUNG S: Here the soul is offered, breathed into the air. It jumps at you from Smetana's river and Dvorak's dance. Let me sing, soar!

> *YOUNG S starts to read a book.*
>
> *MUSICIAN segues to the music for "Wacht auf Verdammte dieser Erde" ("Arise ye damned of this world").*
>
> *A YOUNG RUSSIAN MAN climbs up and down the trucks. He is "limping, bearded... frightening and handsome. Pants torn to fringes, heavy sweater." He comes up to YOUNG S. As he does, SÜSSEL speaks.*

YOUNG S: Sergei. How are you?

SERGEI: *(From on high.)* Russia, beleaguered, needs to be defended. Imagine—socialism begins in a single country. Then in another. And another!

> *Now, having descended, he paces restlessly, going faster and faster, "his voice and crippled leg in rhythm."*

We must make our own revolution here under the leadership, the guidance, of the Great Leader. No need for religion. All injustice will be extinguished! Poverty will be abolished! I promise you, Süssel, that women will be partners, full partners with men! *(He thrusts a publication into her hand.)* Here, read this.

YOUNG S: The Imprecorr. *(He leaves and she reads.)*

SÜSSEL: The forbidden international publication, Imprecorr.

YOUNG S: What a world to come! Not beyond, but on this

	earth here and now. With my help, and without God.
SÜSSEL:	My head spins. I walk on air. Immense power invades my heart. I don't eat, drink, sleep, see anyone, I read Imprecorr. Political, new, something to live and die for.
YOUNG S:	Russia, heaven on earth!

SERGEI comes back, carrying a roll of posters.

SERGEI:	Süssel.
YOUNG S:	Sergei.
SERGEI:	You're going to be leader of a cell of five.
YOUNG S:	I am?
SERGEI:	Yes. And tonight we'll put up posters about the new Worker's Housing Complex.
SÜSSEL:	Ah, the ecstasy of the empowered. It is church without the nonsense.
YOUNG S:	Never, ever have I felt so free, so wonderful, and above all, so right!

MUSICIAN begins to play and SERGEI begins to sing "Der Internationale." YOUNG S joins in. A police whistle. SERGEI hustles off, limp forgotten, leaving YOUNG S alone. POLICEMAN opens a suitcase in which she puts Impreccor. He goes off.

| SÜSSEL: | A policeman goes with me to collect my exam papers, pack my bags, and get me to the train. Foreign students have no rights. I'm deported. |

MUSICIAN plays "Prelude no. 10" from "24 Preludes Op. 38" by Kabalevsky here and at points during the next scene. YOUNG S is left to carry off the suitcase, the roll of posters, and the two chairs. She stomps off with them. Trucks are moved to indicate the entrance to the Strasbourg residence.

SÜSSEL: Back home for the summer, I expect Max to be there, to look up to my window and whistle. But he studies abroad now: physics, astronomy, God knows what, mathematics.

Scene Ten: The Nazi

SÜSSEL: Then...it is late summer. I go to Strasbourg, intending to check into a student residence for well-off girls.

> YOUNG S, *carrying a suitcase, enters. A YOUNG MAN lounges at the entrance. She starts to go by, and he moves into her way.*

YOUNG S: Excuse me.

YOUNG M: You can't go in here.

YOUNG S: Why not?

YOUNG M: You're just a Jew, I know you.

YOUNG S: So?

YOUNG M: I'll have you right here. I'll open my fly, pull your skirt over your head, smear you with the Aryan gift of God, and you'll bear my son and be my Jewish Mary Immaculate. *(He leaves.)*

YOUNG S: *(Turns away.)* No.

> YOUNG S *moves to leave. Fierce music. A swastika appears above her. A voice blares at her, Hitler making a speech. She runs to the other side of the stage. More music. Again, a swastika and part of the speech. She runs to the trucks and climbs them. More music. At the top, she sees another swastika, and the speech finishes with Hitler's audience shouting together,* "Deutschland über alles! Deutschland über alles!"

SÜSSEL: Everyone could see what was going to happen

	as soon as the bloodletting began in Spain. Hitler and Mussolini sent men, planes, and arms to their Fascist friend General Franco right away. To test their war machine. To bomb cities like Guernica into oblivion. The legitimate government had to wait months before Stalin gave them any help. If Spain hadn't fallen in 1939, millions of Jews, millions of others, need not have died.
YOUNG S:	*(She has come back down to the bottom of the trucks and sits.)* Max, Max, where are you? I miss your love for me, as I miss my teenage years. I owned you, could do, say, misbehave as I wished.
SÜSSEL:	I complete my studies. But now my dreams of equality, women's rights, world revolution, lie around me like Master Manole's stones.
SÜSSEL & YOUNG S:	The swastika flies from the rooftops of Germany. Which way, God?

YOUNG S goes off. During SÜSSEL's speech below, she re-enters in white lab coat.

MUSICIAN plays Robert Schumman's "Fast zu ernst" from "Kinderszenen," underscoring the following scene.

Scene Eleven: Back home, and Max

MUSICIAN:	So you're back in Czernowitz…
SÜSSEL:	Working in my father's lab and pharmacy. Twelve hours a day of routine, the practical world, no fancy thoughts. I apply myself to do it right, because in pharmacy no mistakes are allowed. At night I drop dead, my feet burning as if seared on embers. And there is not much thought beyond the working life, no goal. For two years I work.

MAX enters and waits shyly.

YOUNG S: May I help— *(Astonished.)* Max! Max, is it really you?!

MAX: Yes, it's really me.

YOUNG S: It's closing time. Walk me home?

MAX: Of course, Süssel.

YOUNG S takes off her white coat and puts on another, stylish coat. They stroll across the stage. Music stops.

YOUNG S: I can't believe you're back. I thought you were gone for good. You were in Göttingen, right?

MAX: Yes. For five years. Studying mathematics, physics, all theoretical. And where have you been all that time?

YOUNG S: In Prague, in Strasbourg. Sciences and languages. And now I'm here, helping others, healing wounds. What are your plans?

MAX: To return to Göttingen soon and pick up my diplomas. After that, I don't know.

He is silent for a moment.

YOUNG S: What is it, Max?

MAX: I was in the streets on Kristallnacht. I saw stormtroopers with sledge-hammers smashing the windows of Jewish shops. Destroying the synagogue. Beating Jews to death. I got away.

YOUNG S: Thank God.

MAX: Among the German mathematicians I felt safe. Truly, Süssel, they are a better lot than you ordinary scientists.

YOUNG S: Yes, I always suspected you to be of a higher species.

SÜSSEL: Seeing Max again, a little taller perhaps, his neck longer and his forehead higher, but essentially unchanged, makes me giggle.

YOUNG S giggles, and MAX laughs.

MAX: Well, we still have a moment's peace. *(Beat.)* But I think something terrible is going to happen. Something large and terrible. A war is almost here. You must look out for yourself, stay well, Süssel.

YOUNG S: Would you like to come in? Say hello to my mother and father.

MAX: I don't think so. No. I just wanted to see you. Süssel…never…never will I love anyone but you.

He hesitates.

SÜSSEL: Poor Max. He nearly takes me in his arms. But he's too shy.

MAX leaves. YOUNG S stands alone. Music fades out by end of scene.

MUSICIAN: But your world has found its bearings.

SÜSSEL: Yes. Max has returned. Somehow I feel safer.

Scene Twelve: Russians and Germans, June 1940 - October, 1941

Lights down except on SÜSSEL and MUSICIAN. Sound of tanks approaching. Piano is moved from stage left to stage right. Trucks are moved into place to form the walls of the Czernowitz apartment.

SÜSSEL: I remember that sound. Tanks.

MUSICIAN: It is an awful sound.

SÜSSEL:	Perhaps I shouldn't have started this.
MUSICIAN:	The sound of tank treads on cobblestone.
SÜSSEL:	I don't want to remember what happens next.
MUSICIAN:	It's part of the story, isn't it?
SÜSSEL:	I know it's part of the story! I just don't want to remember it.
	Perhaps some things are better forgotten.
MUSICIAN:	Which things?
SÜSSEL:	*(Tartly.)* I'll let you know when I remember them. But this is June, 1940. Hitler has brought all of western Europe to its knees. Jews tremble everywhere.

MUSICIAN begins to play the Soviet national anthem.

The Soviets, the Red Army, moving into Czernowitz, come as saviours, it seems to us.

Sound of tanks louder. Actors stand on trucks and wave small flags..

They drive up the Bahnhofstrasse, in armoured vehicles, tanks the spearhead, to the acclaim of the Jews lining the streets on both sides. Nothing but flowers and smiles for our protectors. But within a year, on a day I can never forget, June 13th, 1941…

Scene Thirteen: Cattle car

Sound of fist pounding on the door. MOTHER in dressing gown. FATHER enters, doing up the belt of his dressing gown. YOUNG S also appears in her dressing gown. A RUSSIAN OFFICER enters.

OFFICER:	*(Points to MOTHER and FATHER.)* You and you! Pack what you can carry! Move! Move!

YOUNG S: What's going on?

OFFICER: Crimes against the Soviet people. *(Shows her paper.)* It's all here.

YOUNG S looks at it.

YOUNG S: "Enemies of the State?" This doesn't make any sense.

OFFICER: It doesn't have to. Stay out of the way, or we'll take you too.

MOTHER and FATHER throw on their coats and take small suitcases.

OFFICER: Move! You sons of bitches! Move!

The OFFICER moves them downstage.

YOUNG S: I'll tell Felix!

MUSICIAN plays "Move!" by Deborah Buck. YOUNG S runs off. As she does so, the OFFICER directs MOTHER and FATHER to get inside a cattle car, crowded with people.

OFFICER: In here. Move!

FATHER: It's a cattle car.

OFFICER: Move!

FATHER: It's already packed.

OFFICER: Move!

MOTHER: There's no room.

OFFICER: Move!

They get in. As he slams the door shut, the piano creates this sound.

Scene Fourteen: Ludmilla

> *On the other side of the stage, FELIX runs in and falls on his knees before LUDMILLA BUNIN, in her dressing robe.*

FELIX: Ludmilla, they've taken my parents. Please, Ludmilla, save them. Telephone the Minister of Health in Kiev, tell her my father is absolutely irreplaceable in his plant. Tell her the workers will perform for him, tell her they adore him. Luditchka, I beg you.

> *LUDMILLA holds out her hands, he rises up, and they embrace. Lights down on them.*

MUSICIAN: Wait! Wait. Who's Ludmilla?

SÜSSEL: Ah, yes, Ludmilla. She's a politruk, a political officer of the Communist Party in the Red Army. I wasn't there, but Felix tells me about her.

> *Lights up on upstage area, with LUDMILLA BUNIN, now in her Soviet Army uniform. FELIX sits in a chair before her. Another SOVIET ARMY OFFICER stands to one side.*

OFFICER: Here is Felix Geller, Comrade Bunin.

BUNIN: Thank you, Comrade. *(To FELIX.)* I am, as I'm sure you know, in charge of all the pharmaceutical industry and retail pharmacies in this area. And thus responsible for correct proletarian behaviour.

FELIX: I know.

BUNIN: And you, I have learned, are one of the worst kinds of capitalist leeches. The same kind of criminal as your father. Real bloodsuckers! Public enemies. We have expropriated both your factory and your pharmacy for the service of the State.

FELIX: I know that too.

BUNIN: But did you know there is inventory missing from both places?

FELIX: I did not do the inventory. I was sent away while your Comrades did it.

BUNIN: Are you suggesting my Comrade soldiers are thieves?

FELIX: I wasn't there. I don't know what they are.

BUNIN: But I know what you are. A liar! Clearly beyond rehabilitation, because of the bourgeoisie you come from. I could send you away to the gulag for ten or twenty years. Just with a word. Do you understand that?

FELIX: Of course.

MUSICIAN: Ah, I see what's needed here.

> *MUSICIAN begins to play a romantic, movie moment piece by Deborah Buck. Lighting effect indicates a movie screen.*

BUNIN: *(To the ARMY OFFICER.)* You are dismissed, Comrade.

OFFICER: Shall I take him?

BUNIN: Not yet, Comrade.

OFFICER: *(Salutes.)* Comrade.

BUNIN: Tell the guard not to let anyone disturb my interrogation of this man.

OFFICER: Comrade. *(He leaves.)*

> *BUNIN and FELIX look at each other. FELIX begins to see that BUNIN has fallen for him. He stands up. They embrace.*

BUNIN: A bourgeois! A class enemy! *(To FELIX.)* I hate you!

FELIX: No, you don't! I don't think someone so beautiful can feel that way.

BUNIN: I hate you! I hate…

FELIX: I love…you.

> *They kiss passionately. The lights on them dim. Music ends.*

MUSICIAN: You're sure this is what happened?

SÜSSEL: It's just how Felix told me.

MUSICIAN: You know this is a young man's version, don't you?

SÜSSEL: I know. It's not very realistic.

MUSICIAN: A young man Hübsch und Schön.

SÜSSEL: And a not very pretty young woman, he tells me.

MUSICIAN: How loyal of him.

SÜSSEL: But useful.

MUSICIAN: She saves your mother and father.

SÜSSEL: From perhaps ten thousand deportees.

MUSICIAN: So they come home. *(Plays "Move!" fading during opening of scene.)*

SÜSSEL: Home…what's left of it.

Scene Fifteen: Grief

> *Lights up on the apartment, as FATHER and MOTHER enter, helped by YOUNG S.*

MOTHER: It is nothing, my child, it is nothing, we're home.

> *MOTHER slumps down on one chair. FATHER falls into another.*

SÜSSEL: My father, his face ashen, unshaven, says with utter derision:

FATHER: So much for your communistic liberators.

SÜSSEL: I understand, he's speaking to me. *(Beat.)* It takes three days to get them out. The cattle car packed with people, and just one small window, criss-crossed by iron, high up near the ceiling. When they get home, I fall to the floor, to undo the laces of my father's shoes. *(YOUNG S does this.)* His underpants full of his waste, he sleeps on the chair he's fallen into, next to my mother.

> *YOUNG S sits down in the middle of the floor, head in hands. After a moment, her father cries out from his sleep, "a savage sound of grief." YOUNG S tries to take his hand but he waves her away.*

Scene Sixteen: Kaddish

SÜSSEL: This is going to get worse.

MUSICIAN: Do you need to rest?

SÜSSEL: No. Not yet. Though I feel like Master Manole's wife, trapped in a small, breathless space by all these memories. Maybe that's why I keep hearing her scream. Maybe this will help me break free.

MUSICIAN: Yes. What do you remember next?

> *Approaching German soldiers indicated by piano music,"Nazi March" by Deborah Buck, and actors' marching feet, becoming louder.*

SÜSSEL: It's just a few weeks later, at the end of June, 1941. We know the Germans are on their way. The Russians leave, Ludmilla with them. My father tells Felix to run for it. And he does. I don't know where. East somewhere.

Sound of rifle butts on doors. Glass smashing. Orders shouted by a German officer.

OFFICER: Alle Juden müssen raus auf die Strasse! Alle Juden müssen raus—sofort!

In their third-floor apartment, MOTHER, FATHER, and YOUNG S wait in fear, as the sounds of boots clambering up stairs and shouts come closer.

YOUNG S: *(Whispers.)* Are they going to come up here?

FATHER: *(Whispers.)* Let's hope not.

OFFICER: Hier ist einer! Schiessen! Noch Einer! Raus sofort!

Sound of screams and shots nearby.

MOTHER: *(Muffled.)* No! No!

Closer screams and shots.

YOUNG S: They're on the floor just below.

MOTHER: The last judgement, no more days to come.

OFFICER: Halt! Schiessen, verdamnt! Alle! Alle!

A moment of silence.

Kein Zeit! Los! Weiter!

Boots thunder down stairs. Silence and lights down to dim.

YOUNG S: I think they've gone.

FATHER: Let's see if we can help.

MUSICIAN plays the melody of "Kaddisch" from "Deux Melodies Hébraiques" by Maurice Ravel. In the half-light, MOTHER, FATHER, and YOUNG S discover bodies (chairs, trunks, and suitcases) and take them towards the walnut tree.

MOTHER: Who is this?

FATHER: Our grocer. Old Lev-Jossel Green.

MOTHER: And this in his arms?

YOUNG S: His youngest child, Lisa.

FATHER: Let them rest under the walnut tree until we've dug a grave.

> *Spot up on SÜSSEL. Motions of digging in background.*

SÜSSEL: Oh, our walnut tree, broad and outreaching, sheltering, its top branches touching the clouds, a dreamworld lost in its foliage, now all these dreams lying under it.

FATHER: We can't dig here. The roots rebel.

YOUNG S: The tree doesn't want our bodies.

FATHER: We'll have to bury them in the garden.

> *MARUSJA enters to help.*

MOTHER: Marusja, is that you?

MARUSJA: Yes.

MOTHER: And Dmitry?

MARUSJA: We locked the door to our cellar room when the soldiers came. He's still there.

MOTHER: Ah.

> *They finish piling bodies up.*

SÜSSEL: Christian neighbours come to help us dig and bury the bodies. No cloth, no linen, just earth to earth and covered with earth. We say the Kaddish and our Gentile helpers repeat the ancient Aramaic words with us:

	Praised be and glorified.
	MOTHER, FATHER, YOUNG S, MARUSJA and others murmur the Kaddish.
ALL:	Magnified and sanctified is God's great name throughout the whole World of Creation. May God's sovereignty be accepted in our lives and the lives of the People Israel and all peoples, soon and in our days, and let us say: "Amen." *(Music ends.)*
SÜSSEL:	We don't see the blood until the sun rises.
SÜSSEL & MUSICIAN:	Blood on our hands, faces, clothes, and shoes.
MUSICIAN:	And then…
SÜSSEL:	By early October all of us Jews from Czernowitz are jammed into the Ghetto. My mother and Grandmother Esther are just on the other side of a room, but can't cross it. There are fifty people between us, sitting on suitcases and bundles.
	On one side of the pile of suitcases and trunks, MOTHER sits on a black leather bag with brass buckles. On the other side, FATHER and YOUNG S sit on their own suitcases.

Scene Seventeen: Uniform

SÜSSEL:	Ah, but I'm forgetting. Before that, before the ghetto, Marusja's husband, Dmitry, who has been away, returns. In a German uniform. I see him arrive. Go to listen at the cellar door.
	MARUSJA is setting a just-baked loaf of bread down. DMITRY enters in a German uniform. YOUNG S listens at the door.
MARUSJA:	Dmitry! Dmitry! *(She embraces him.)*
DMITRY:	Oh, your heavenly bread, Marusjenka!

MARUSJA: Welcome home.

> *He rips off some of the hot crust, eats it, and kisses her three times. She steps back.*

MARUSJA: A German uniform? Why are you wearing a German uniform?

DMITRY: I have a Ukrainian heart. I want a little glory for my people.

MARUSJA: And what glory, Dmitry? What is this thing I've never heard of before? Except for the glory of God, all glories are for the devil. Go to your father's, work the fields, hide when the soldiers come to fetch you. Who will look after your little Marusja?

DMITRY: I will. I won't let my little one starve, but I cannot stay home when all Ukrainian men are joining the army, one or the other, Russian or German. If we join early, we'll be in on the German victory, which is a sure thing!

MARUSJA: How sure? All I can see is that the world is upside down. They're after the Jews now but the Ukrainians will be next. The Germans do not respect us. I don't trust them. Dmitry, go home and hide!

DMITRY: The Jews have plundered us as long as we can remember, now we'll take some of it back. The days of reckoning have come. Let them die, they're an accursed race, they killed Christ, they suck our blood.

MARUSJA: My grandmother said, "Do not touch the Jews, let them be. God has chosen them. God has chosen his Son among them. He has chosen them to crucify Him. For us, for us. The Jews have done it for us, to lighten the burden of our sins."

DMITRY: I must go, Marusjenka. I'm the leader of a small platoon.

MARUSJA: So soon?

DMITRY: Kiss me goodbye, Marusjenka. Don't worry, my angel, I'll be back for you.

MARUSJA: Then God bless you. May Saint Cyril and all the angels watch over you. And one more thing, Dmitry, swear you won't—

DMITRY: I swear.

> *He kisses her hurriedly, grabs the loaf of bread, and leaves. Lights down on them.*

Scene Eighteen: Doctor Hermann Bauer

MUSICIAN: After that you all get taken to the Ghetto.

SÜSSEL: Yes, soon after that. I hear that Max is there, but I don't see him. It's not long before my father and I are requisitioned to work in a German field hospital. We have to leave Mother and Grandmother Esther behind.

> *Field Hospital music—MUSICIAN improvises on a few phrases of "La Séparation" from "Chants Populaires Hébraique" by Darius Milaud. This underscores all except the MUSICIAN/ SÜSSEL scenes that follow.*
>
> *Trucks are moved to form the lab in the field hospital. YOUNG S, FATHER, and one OTHER PHARMACIST wear lab coats with yellow stars on them. MAJOR DR. HERMANN BAUER impatiently enters. He has a duelling scar on one cheek, which also distorts his lip.*

SÜSSEL: We're there to serve the young German boys—shot, amputated, delirious, dying for a madman's cause.

BAUER: So this is what they send me for my hospital lab. Jews from the ghetto. How many of you are there?

YOUNG S: Six, with degrees in Pharmacy.

BAUER: Degrees? Degrees from where?

YOUNG S: Strasbourg. Vienna. Prague.

> *YOUNG S, unwashed and unfed, can hardly stand on her feet. But BAUER is at once "astounded" by her.*

BAUER: What did you do with these degrees?

YOUNG S: I was in charge of my father's pharmacy in Czernowitz.

BAUER: *(To FATHER.)* And you?

FATHER: *(Terrified.)* I...I ran a...pharmaceutical factory.

BAUER: *(To YOUNG S.)* You can be in charge of my laboratory. The head Jew. Someone to co-ordinate between the lab and the ward. Feldscher. We have hundreds of wounded German boys from the front to deal with. *(To OTHER PHARMACIST.)* I need anaesthesia. Morphine.

YOUNG S & FATHER: We can do all that.

BAUER: Good. I need it now. Right now.

> *He turns to leave. YOUNG S seizes the moment.*

YOUNG S: Herr Doctor?

BAUER: Yes?

YOUNG S: A work team has just arrived from Moghilev.

BAUER: To build more barracks. I know.

YOUNG S: May I be permitted to requisition one of them to clean our latrines?

BAUER: I suppose he's a relative.

YOUNG S: It would mean we could spend more time in the lab.

BAUER: No. Not from that team. They're full of fleas and typhus. I'll keep your father and you...but watch out. Now...get to work. *(He strides off.)*

YOUNG S: *(Beat.)* Poor uncle Saul.

FATHER: You tried to save him.

YOUNG S: I wonder what has happened to Mother and Grandmother Esther.

FATHER: Who can know?

YOUNG S: I hope they're all right.

FATHER: Only God knows if they are. We'd better get to work.

> *Light and music transition. FATHER, YOUNG S and OTHER at the lab bench, working. BAUER enters.*

BAUER: I've just got a shipment of live mercury I need turned into ointment.

FATHER: We'll need some medium to mix it in. Lanolin or pork fat would be best.

BAUER: Jews wanting pork? *(Laughs.)* Anyway, we don't have any.

YOUNG S: How about vaseline?

BAUER: That we have.

FATHER: We'll mix equal quantities to start, then slowly incorporate more vaseline.

BAUER: Good. Good.

FATHER: I'll go.

FATHER leaves. BAUER fixes YOUNG S with his gaze.

SÜSSEL: Ha! The crucial moment. Now where is that letter?

Opens the drawers of the bed, rapidly searching.

MUSICIAN: What letter?

SÜSSEL: The letter from the condom.

MUSICIAN: From the condom?

SÜSSEL: I'm sure it's here somewhere.

MUSICIAN: And the letter is from?

SÜSSEL: Dr. Bauer of course. *(She finds it, squares of shiny, harsh toilet paper.)* Aha! Here it is. Listen. *(Begins to read.)* "Forgive me. This is my letter to you. I am writing it on toilet paper and will roll it into a condom. A letter of penance, maybe, but also of confession." *(Flipping pages.)* And so on. So on.

SÜSSEL: "You may not believe me, but I knew you from the moment your green eyes met mine."

MUSICIAN: And how do you feel?

SÜSSEL: There's no escape for me. I am nothing, just a Jew in servitude, and he can take me by command.

BAUER goes to the bed and sits down on a trunk at its end.

BAUER: I knew you from the moment your green eyes met mine. You Jews are nothing to me. I've never known one before. They say Jews harm our very social fabric. The Bible seems to say that. I come from church-going Catholics, grew up in a forester's home in the Sylva Nigra, the Schwarzwald. Hospitals are far away, and God's will is accepted in our home. But I'm clever and get sent to medical school.

Know Jews? I don't even know any Protestants. Nothing of politics either. Catechism. Mass on Sundays. Prayer, work, and the sublime forest, touching the clouds, rooted.

In her eighth childbed, my mother dies. I fall in love with the newly-born. Of such utter beauty, rose-petal skin and eyes green as emerald. Your eyes that strike me suddenly.

FATHER turns to where BAUER is seated.

FATHER: Dr. Bauer?

BAUER: *(Moving to them.)* What is it now?

FATHER: Our patients are starting to show signs of scurvy. They need Vitamin C.

BAUER: I know that. But we don't have any.

FATHER: We can make some. If we go out into the fields—with guards of course—we can collect frozen rosehips from under the snow.

BAUER: You know where to collect Hagebutten?

FATHER: Yes. Then we simply have to let them defrost and boil them into an extract.

BAUER: Full of Vitamin C. A very good idea...Herr Geller.

FATHER: Thank you.

BAUER: You have my permission.

YOUNG S: Thank you.

FATHER leaves, and YOUNG S starts to follow.

BAUER: *(To YOUNG S.)* Wait.

MUSICIAN: *(Stops playing "Field Hospital music".)* I can see where this is going.

SÜSSEL:	Of course you can. So can I. But I want something.
MUSICIAN:	Of course you do.
SÜSSEL:	And not what you might think.

BAUER comes close to SÜSSEL.

BAUER:	Sleep…with me…tonight.
YOUNG S:	Why?
BAUER:	You'll have dinner and wine, and I'll let you rest in my quarters for a day.
YOUNG S:	Is this an order?
BAUER:	You are clever and know me now well enough, you know I will be good to you.
YOUNG S:	Yes, I do know. But may I respectfully ask for a favour?
BAUER:	A favour?
YOUNG S:	Yes. Bring my fiancé out of the ghetto.
BAUER:	Your fiancé? What is his name?
YOUNG S:	Max. Max Birnbaum.
BAUER:	*(Pause.)* All right.

BAUER leaves. MUSICIAN plays "Ch'bin A Bocher, A Hultay" ("I'm a Wandering Fellow"), a Jewish folk melody, as YOUNG S runs off to go to the ghetto.

Scene Nineteen: Max in the ghetto

MAX, on one side of a crowd of people. YOUNG S enters. They can't reach each other and have to shout. Music underscores this scene.

YOUNG S:	Max, are you there? Max?
MAX:	Süssel! Are they sending you back here?
YOUNG S:	No. I have a letter from my boss, Doctor Bauer. To get you released.
MAX:	I'm being released? Thank you, Süssel. How are you?
YOUNG S:	I'm fine. And you?
MAX:	I...I think of you often.
YOUNG S:	I have to go.
MAX:	Wait!
YOUNG S:	*(Calls back.)* Goodbye, Max.
MAX:	Süssel...
YOUNG S:	Goodbye!
MAX:	Süssel...*(To himself.)*...farewell.

Music pauses. MAX stands there, uncertain where to go.

Which way to turn? Which way to turn now?

MAX goes off. Music ends.

SÜSSEL:	I didn't know if I'd ever see him again.
MUSICIAN:	But Doctor Bauer keeps his word.
SÜSSEL:	Yes. Max gets out of the ghetto. But soon enough the Germans recapture him and send him to a work camp.
MUSICIAN:	I'm sorry.
SÜSSEL:	I did what I could.

MUSICIAN: And do you know what happens to him after that?

SÜSSEL: Not really. I wasn't there.

MUSICIAN: Will this help?

> *MUSICIAN plays a Jewish folk melody, "Yoshke Fort Avek" ("Yoshke's Leaving Now"), underscoring the following scene.*

SÜSSEL: Yes, it will. Thank you.

Scene Twenty: Joey and Helen

> *Lights up on MAX and JOEY sitting huddled together, resting against three chairs in a pile, under an ankle-length, threadbare, Russian soldier's coat. MAX has a fever.*

MAX: *(Shakes and moans.)* Oh, look at my fingers. They're as white as the snowfields. My tongue is on fire, my eyeballs are jumping from their orbits. Give me a drink, Joey!

JOEY: *(Gives him a drink.)* Here, take this. You're getting better, your fever is down. Tomorrow you can work again. Just don't die on me.

MAX: Where's Grisha?

JOEY: He's already asleep. He's fine.

MAX: Good.

MUSICIAN: Grisha? Who's Grisha?

SÜSSEL: There's no time for him now.

JOEY: Anyway, Max, I haven't finished telling you about Helen.

MAX: You know there's a five o'clock roll call. If we're not up—

JOEY:	I love the smell rising from under her armpits! The crude French words she loves to say and hear, her habit of turning away to feel my rising desire against her backside, all the little beauty spots on her neck and breasts, her night-smell, her dishevelled hair.
MAX:	You don't have to tell me all this.
JOEY:	Yes! I do! I do. It helps me to remember. And I think she's safe where I left her. But she's going to have our child any day. I'm afraid I'm never going to see her again, or the child.
MAX:	Joey, let's sleep now, or we won't be strong enough to stand on our feet at roll call. They'll shoot us if we can't work.
JOEY:	But Max, she's too beautiful, too vulnerable to face it all alone.
MAX:	Joey, I will find Helen and look after her if you cannot. Let's sleep now, my friend, my brother.
JOEY:	If you do, remember, praise her for everything. She does not live by bread alone, she lives by praise. Her eyes will brighten and with her hands she'll fix a strand of her hair self-consciously, over her ears. Praise her, Max.
MAX:	I will. I promise you I will. Joey, mine own. I'll find her, you know. Helen. I will find her.
JOEY:	That's good, Max. Let's both sleep now.

Music stops. Lights down on them. They exit.

MUSICIAN:	Was it that bad?
SÜSSEL:	It must have been even worse.
MUSICIAN:	At least they had friendship.
SÜSSEL:	It's true. Even love, I think.

MUSICIAN: Now, what about you and Doctor Bauer?

> *"Field Hospital" music underscores all except MUSICIAN/ SÜSSEL scenes in the following.*

SÜSSEL: After I get Max out of the ghetto?

MUSICIAN: Yes.

Scene Twenty-One: Love

> *DR. BAUER carries in a tray of chocolate and apricots and sets it on the bed. He smoothes the army blanket, then leaves. After a moment, YOUNG S enters.*

SÜSSEL: His barracks are fifty metres from the hospital, somewhere in heaven.

YOUNG S: Ah, apricots. And chocolate! *(Eats something.)*

> *She takes off her prison garb, undresses to slip and panties, drapes the outer clothing over the headboard, gets into bed, and collapses into sleep.*

SÜSSEL: I sleep countless hours.

> *DR. BAUER enters quietly, takes her prison garb, and leaves.*

He returns to wake me at four-thirty in the morning, my sterilized clothes in his arms; he has operated all night.

> *DR. BAUER enters, with a tray on top of her folded clothes. YOUNG S wakes up.*

YOUNG S: Coffee!

DR. BAUER: And bread and butter. *(He gives her the tray.)*

YOUNG S: *(As BAUER leaves.)* Thank you.

MUSICIAN: So no sex.

SÜSSEL:	Did I say there was sex?
MUSICIAN:	No.
SÜSSEL:	If there's sex, I'll tell you.
MUSICIAN:	All right. And after that?
SÜSSEL:	It's all in this letter.
MUSICIAN:	The one from the condom.
SÜSSEL:	Yes. Listen. *(She starts to read.)*

DOCTOR BAUER stands near the bed.

SÜSSEL & BAUER: "You are mine, and I will make you mine, slowly."

BAUER: I am not a very sexual man. I dream of things, but I do not make them come true. Then, as if heaven-sent, in a no-place, no-man's land, by God almost, I learn to love.

I want to earn you, as an equal would. I could have ordered you to my bed. But I want to see if you are honourable.

(Beat.) Why do I tremble, shiver, before a slave whose life I can extinguish with a wink of my eyelash?

A PRISONER brings BAUER a basin of hot water and a surgical brush, washcloth and towel. YOUNG S enters, sees the basin.

YOUNG S: Hot water!

She takes off her lab coat and dress and sits on the trunk at the end of the bed. DR. BAUER kneels on the bed, soaks the washcloth and drips water over her head. Then he takes a surgical brush and slowly scrubs her head. Finally, he blots the water with the towel, leaving it around her hair.

BAUER: Your hair, when grown again, will be beautiful.

DR. BAUER carries the basin, cloth, brush and towel off. YOUNG S gets into bed.

Music ends.

MUSICIAN: So still no sex?

SÜSSEL: Why this obsession with sex?

MUSICIAN: It just seems it would be normal.

SÜSSEL: There's nothing normal about this situation.

MUSICIAN: As you say.

YOUNG S is sleeping. DR. BAUER enters and stands at the head of the bed, then moves to kneel near its side, watching YOUNG S.

BAUER: I wait. But there is no time, the war is moving faster now. This time, which curtails itself so rapidly, is our time. But you love me, love me. You guess what I am. Guess that I want your body and soul, pure as virginal snow. Want to be found, rescued, and owned. Life created, exhaled into you almost, by me alone.

SÜSSEL: I love him furiously. His face, his duelled sharp Schmiss across his right cheek, his distorted upper lip, his eyebrows, those celestial arcs, are with me everywhere.

BAUER: *(Rising.)* As you become flesh of my flesh and let me pour you into my form, you allow me my manhood.

SÜSSEL: I am pursued by his face. Mad, mad, I love him.

"YOUNG S Wakes" music by Deborah Buck. As BAUER moves towards the bed, YOUNG S stands up on it.

BAUER: You give me that gift. It could be for a day's rest, for a meal of sausage and sauerkraut, or simply for a basin of warm water to wash in. But it is not, it is love. Love that allows me to fashion you, so you can live within my fibre. My hand's artefact, my child, my new-born sister.

SÜSSEL: He comes to me fully aroused one morning at four-thirty and takes me without warning.

> *Piano chord, as YOUNG S and BAUER embrace and cry out.*

Catatonic as he wants me, the thrill will ring through my life.

BAUER: *(He lets her down to stand facing him.)* Do you love me?

YOUNG S & SÜSSEL: I love you.

> *Music ends. They exit in separate directions.*

MUSICIAN: So that's the sex... Such as it was.

SÜSSEL: Such as it was. The sex isn't important. Love is.

MUSICIAN: So, what about Max?

SÜSSEL: Max?

MUSICIAN: Yes, Max. Your fiancé.

SÜSSEL: Something like this.

> *MUSICIAN improvises on "Yoshke Fort Avek."*

Scene Twenty-Two: Escape

> *Lights up on MAX and JOEY.*

JOEY: *(Softly, urgently.)* Max! Max! Wake up.

MAX: Joey! What is it?

JOEY: Wake up.

MAX: Is it time to work already?

JOEY: No. It's midnight.

MAX: Midnight?

JOEY: The orders are here for tomorrow morning. The camp is to be annihilated. The Romanian guard told me. None will survive.

MAX: What can we do?

JOEY: We may be shot. But we have to run. If we get across the river, we'll be safe. Come, we must run!

MAX and JOEY run off.

MUSICIAN: And what about you?

SÜSSEL: This is how we learned.

FATHER stands before BAUER, who has a paper in his hand. MUSICIAN starts to weave in a phrase from "Prelude 10" from "24 Preludes" by Kabalevsky.

BAUER: I have orders from the Command. *(He crumples the paper.)* But here is what you must do. You and the other staff. You must run.

FATHER: We must run?

BAUER: I will be on duty. There are no dogs anymore. There will be no guards.

FATHER: But the sick German boys?

BAUER: They will be shipped on trucks, tanks, and go on foot. It is none of your concern.

FATHER: It is my concern.

BAUER: It is not. Look out for yourselves. Take the Russian coats, fur hats, and boots. *(Takes rucksack from under the bed.)* Here is a small rucksack with what I could spare. Take your daughter. In thirty minutes move silently out of the compound. Direction southwest. Hurry.

FATHER: Thank you.

BAUER: One moment more—shake my hand. I have never before seen a war hero of your stature.

They shake hands. Preceding music builds to furious river sound and underscores during a long cloth being moved across upstage, lit to suggest the river. MAX, JOEY and OTHERS are behind it, shouting to each other.

OTHERS: We'll never make it!

JOEY: Here's the river! Quick, kick off your boots! They'll pull you down.

MAX: The water's too deep, the current—

OTHERS: No, no, it's too cold!

JOEY: Max, come on! Grisha, come on!

MAX: Joey, help me. I'm afraid!

JOEY: Come on, Max, my friend! Come on, Grisha!

MAX: The water's so cold!

They wade into the river. Shots. JOEY is hit.

JOEY: I'm hit! Keep going, Max!

MAX: No! No! Try!

JOEY: Remember your promise!

MAX: What?

JOEY: Helen. Your promise. *(He drowns.)*

MAX & OTHERS: Joey!

MAX: Grisha? Where are you? Grisha!

Music fades as river calms, and morphs into fragments of Robert Schumman's "Träumerei," as DOCTOR BAUER speaks. Sound of blizzard begins and grows during his speech. Lighting on cloth changes to indicate snow.

YOUNG S and FATHER, exhausted and weak, in heavy Russian coats and fur hats, struggle through strong wind and thick snow. FATHER stumbles to the ground.

BAUER: The chance that you will survive this bitter winter, you and your father, is almost non-existent. These words, then, are just to relive, rethink, and give account. To face also the experience, the elemental nature of our love. You may be robbed, beaten.

SÜSSEL: Or you may huddle against the small cove of a windbreak and just sleep in the snow.

BOTH: So it is a farewell.

BAUER exits, carrying the trunk. Lights down on FATHER and YOUNG S.

SÜSSEL: I'm so tired. So tired.

MUSICIAN: It's going well. You can rest now.

SÜSSEL: *(Lying down.)* I will. We'll carry on again later.

Music ends. Blackout.

End of Act I.

Act II

Scene Twenty-Three: Mother and Marusja

The MUSICIAN again begins to play fragments of Robert Schumman's "Träumerei" ("Dreaming"). Lights up on SÜSSEL, asleep.

Once more, figures appear briefly in the background. They are her FATHER, who does not speak and turns his back, FELIX, whose left leg is missing, so he has a limp and carries a cane, MARUSJA, LUDMILLA, MAX, and her MOTHER. MOTHER's hair is now silver. She wears a grey silk dress under a Russian coat. She carries the black leather bag with brass buckles.

MOTHER: A mother must save the world.

MARUSJA: I love these linked, shining trees.

FELIX: She saved us all.

LUDMILLA: He is my husband forever.

MAX: I have to go on a journey.

SÜSSEL stirs, calls out softly, longingly.

SÜSSEL: Mother.

MOTHER enters the apartment. It's been looted. A few books are strewn about the floor, some still in a bookcase. MARUSJA appears.

MARUSJA: You're back! I thought I heard footsteps.

MOTHER: Marusja! Oh, Marusja.

> *MARUSJA rushes to greet MOTHER. They embrace.*

MOTHER: I didn't know if you'd still be here. And Dmitry?

MARUSJA: He hasn't returned.

MOTHER: Perhaps he'll still…

MARUSJA: Perhaps.

MOTHER: Your family?

MARUSJA: No word.

MOTHER: I'm sorry. *(Looks around.)* What have the Germans left?

MARUSJA: Some blankets. Pillows. Some dishes.

MOTHER: And some books. *(Picks them up.)* Shakespeare…Verlaine…Rimbaud. Furniture does not make a home, books do. I'm at home.

MARUSJA: I'll get some soup. Bean soup. And fresh bread.

MOTHER: My god, fresh bread. Thank you.

> *MARUSJA rushes out to get the food. MOTHER sits at the window seat and looks out the window. Lights down on MOTHER.*
>
> *Music stops. SÜSSEL wakes up.*

SÜSSEL: *(To MUSICIAN.)* Was I sleeping long?

MUSICIAN: No, not long. Did you sleep well?

SÜSSEL: *(Surprised.)* Yes, I did.

MUSICIAN: So you didn't hear anyone screaming?

SÜSSEL: No. There was no screaming. But…my mother…

MUSICIAN: Yes?

SÜSSEL: It must have been 1944. Early 1944. Spring. The war goes on elsewhere. But the Russians have taken control of Czernowitz once more. I dreamed...I dreamed about my mother being home.

SÜSSEL takes up her writing pad and pen. She begins to write rapidly.

MUSICIAN: And where are you?

SÜSSEL: In Bucharest. I made it to Bucharest.

MUSICIAN: And your father?

SÜSSEL: Don't ask. Don't ask. Right now, this is about my mother.

MUSICIAN: All right.

SÜSSEL: Someone comes to see her.

Scene Twenty-Four: Mother and Ludmilla

MUSICIAN begins to play a Russian folk melody, "Tumbalalaika," cut off by:

SÜSSEL: No, stop. I don't need that. I know exactly what happens. My mother tells me all about this.

Lights up on MOTHER making tea on a small alcohol burner. MOTHER hears someone approaching.

MOTHER: Marusja?

LUDMILLA BUNIN, in her Soviet Army uniform with coat and hat, appears.

Ah, you've come to take over the apartment.

LUDMILLA: What?

MOTHER: I assume you've been assigned to this apartment. That's fine. I'll leave.

LUDMILLA: No. Not at all.

MOTHER: Then how may I help you?

LUDMILLA: You're Mrs. Geller, aren't you? The mother of Felix Geller?

MOTHER: Yes.

LUDMILLA: Felix showed me your photograph.

MOTHER: Why would he do that?

LUDMILLA: After I saved you. You and your husband.

MOTHER: Saved me? How?

LUDMILLA: You don't know? Felix didn't tell you about us?

MOTHER: No.

LUDMILLA: Oh.

MOTHER: But please tell me now.

LUDMILLA: I had better tell you, because... Well, during the deportation Felix came running to me, breathless and desperate, and cried, "Help us, help us, your soldiers have taken my father and mother into the trains." I kissed his tears, and ran to my office. We, the politruks—you know, Mrs. Geller, we, the political officers of the Party, we have power. I phoned Kiev and managed to get a stay of deportation. It took three days, but I brought you home.

MOTHER: *(Astonished.)* So you saved our lives. I thank you. But what is your name?

LUDMILLA: My name? Oh, I'm sorry. I'm Ludmilla, Ludmilla Bunin.

MOTHER: Thank you, Ludmilla Bunin.

LUDMILLA pulls out a cameo, with a small passport photo of FELIX in it, hung on a chain under her uniform.

LUDMILLA: See this.

MOTHER: It's a photograph of my Felix.

LUDMILLA: Yes. I wear it always. I came because I have to find him.

MOTHER: I'm sorry, I don't know where he is.

LUDMILLA: You don't know? I had hoped...

MOTHER: Let's have tea.

She pours tea for them both. They talk and sip tea.

LUDMILLA: I've come all the way from Vladivostok, the other side of the country, on an army train across Siberia, with two words to guide me: Czernowitz and Felix.

MOTHER: You've come such a long way.

LUDMILLA: It took months. Now I have two days of leave. Only two.

MOTHER: Why don't you stay with me? I have no beds, but there are blankets and some pillows.

LUDMILLA: I don't need a bed.

MOTHER: Then it will give me great pleasure to have you as my guest. They have permitted me to stay until someone comes to fetch me. If they ever do.

LUDMILLA: Someone will. Felix was so good to me. He kissed my hand and called me his lady love, told me I was getting prettier day by day because he said so.

MOTHER: Yes, I believe my son knows how to see a woman's beauty.

LUDMILLA: And Felix...Felix would meet me after work, in the headquarters of the NKVD—the Secret Police. I was the officer in charge. We met night after night. Your son has loved and taught me love of my body. My ugliness vanished. He said, "I have had sex with the loveliest women, but Ludmilla, see your shining face! No one has ever given me that." And now he is my husband forever. I have been married to him!

MOTHER: Married? How can that be, if you haven't seen him for so long?

LUDMILLA: I don't mean in the usual way. Of course, he wasn't even there. But truly we are married. You see, in Russia now, we are forbidden to think of God. We are only allowed to think of Father Stalin, Father Lenin, and Father Marx. But my people are Christians, the old Orthodox true faith. So I went to my brother, Gregory, a clandestine priest of the Russian Orthodox Church, and I said, "Marry me to this man." You see, Mother—I hope I may call you Mother now—

MOTHER: Of course.

LUDMILLA: These were Stalingrad days. Hard days, when men's lives were—well, Russians understand. Gregory covered his head, took the liturgy in hand, set a crown on my head, spoke the blessing. He was priest and bridegroom for me.

MOTHER: I see.

LUDMILLA: You have taught Felix the true faith, even if you are not in the church: love will save the world. Mothers will save the world, you and Mathka Bohu, the mother of Jesus.

MOTHER: I hope with all my heart that you find Felix.

LUDMILLA: Thank you, my dear Mother. And if I never find my Felix, I'll work as long as strength permits and then I'll give my life to God. My brother has found a Siberian monastery, unknown to the régime. A commune, true to the spirit of the Russian Church. Old style: a sharing of bread, of work, a holy place. And this is what I will do. But first, I cry before you as Felix did before me on that night: Mother, help me find him!

MOTHER: Dear Ludmilla, perhaps you carry the message from God: a mother must save the world. Through love, she will save the world. Then, for all our sons and lovers, I will help you. Who will, if not I?

LUDMILLA: That is all I ask. I'll leave you the name of the monastery village. Thank you.

MOTHER: Rest now, my daughter.

LUDMILLA: I'm so glad I found you.

> *They embrace. MUSICIAN underscores the following with "Prelude no. 17" from "24 Preludes Op 38" by Kabalevsky, which morphs into a church bell effect.*

SÜSSEL: After her two days, Ludmilla has to go. And I never meet her. I wish I had. I wonder if she makes it to the monastery in Siberia. What happens to this woman who chooses love instead of power?

MUSICIAN: "Love will save the world."

SÜSSEL: My Mother waits and waits. Still no Felix, still no Süssel.

Scene Twenty-Five: Mother and Marusja

> *MOTHER sits on the window seat looking out. MARUSJA enters. Church bells fade.*

MARUSJA: It's Easter Sunday. Come with me to midnight mass?

MOTHER: Thank you, no, dear Marusja. I might miss Süssel. You know how impatient she can be. *(They smile.)* You know, I often wanted to hold her close, protect her, but she ran from me. Pushed away, mocked my love. Or so I thought. But now I know she will come. Or perhaps my son Felix. And Marusja…

MARUSJA: Yes?

MOTHER: I thank you for your love. I fear there won't be time to speak when they come to fetch me. I may go without knocking at your door. It will be easier that way. Marusja, you showed me a love I had not expected and do not think I deserved.

MARUSJA: Please, don't…

MOTHER: Marusja, dear, this is a woman's bond. We give birth. We know love. Beyond measure, call, or duty. I've seen you in servitude to us and I've also seen your love to Dmitry. It was truly incomprehensible to me at the time. Because I'm proud. But I have learnt. And now I thank you, for that bond between us. Now remember this. Come after I am gone, as quickly as you can and take the carpets. That's all that's left. Come and take them before others do.

MARUSJA: Thank you. I will come.

> *A bit more of "Prelude no. 17". MARUSJA exits.*

MUSICIAN: *(To SÜSSEL.)* You're getting quite good at telling this story. You weren't even there, but it all seems so true.

SÜSSEL: As I said, my mother tells me everything.

MUSICIAN: So you find her, of course. *(Fade in "Lechayim," a Jewish folk melody.)*

SÜSSEL: Yes. I don't know she's in Czernowitz, but I pay some Bucharest smugglers to take me there and bring us back if I find her. It's September of 1944. The Germans have left Romania. Of course, they bomb Bucharest before they leave. *(Music ends.)*

Scene Twenty-Six: Mother and Süssel

MOTHER is asleep on the window seat. YOUNG S arrives.

YOUNG S: Mother!

MOTHER: *(Waking.)* Süssel? Süssel! Sweetie!

YOUNG S and MOTHER embrace.

YOUNG S: I found you, I found you!

MOTHER: Wait. How is Father? Where is he?

SÜSSEL & YOUNG S: Don't ask me that now.

YOUNG S: There's no time.

MUSICIAN: Why wouldn't you tell her?

SÜSSEL & YOUNG S: Later, I'll tell you later. Please?

MUSICIAN & MOTHER: All right. Later.

MOTHER: I'm just so happy to see you.

During the above, YOUNG S helps MOTHER into her Russian coat and takes her bag.

YOUNG S:	Come with me now. A truck is waiting to take us to Bucharest. I found Felix there.
MOTHER:	You found Felix!
YOUNG S:	He's lost a leg. Shattered by a bullet, it had to be amputated.
MOTHER:	Lost a leg? Oh, dear.
YOUNG S:	But he's alive, he's well. Come!
MOTHER:	Wait. Let me look out the window one last time.

> *MUSICIAN plays more of "Prelude no. 17," as MOTHER goes to the window with YOUNG S and they look out. They exit. Music fades under:*

Scene Twenty-Seven: The Tree of Life

> *After a moment, MARUSJA appears and looks around.*

MARUSJA: Let the Russians have these rooms. I won't move into them. Jews have been killed and God would punish me. Let the locusts sleep in their beds, not me. *(Beat.)* The carpets, she said to take the carpets. *(Goes to the "Tree of Life" carpet, takes it down, and caresses it as she speaks.)* I love these linked, shining trees. They make you tremble. Not like the Romanian lady, Master Manole's wife, walled in for the glory of God, who screams for air and does not get it. This is different. Life from the top of the tree to the root of the next. Birds singing in their branches.

> *MUSICIAN plays "In One Spot" (Dance no. 3) from "Romanian Folk Dances" by Bela Bartok, as MARUSJA rolls up the carpet and hoists it under her arm. She also takes the soup tureen from where it's hidden. She exits.*

Scene Twenty-Eight: Mother, Süssel, and Felix

MOTHER and FELIX sit on suitcases. He holds MOTHER's hands. YOUNG S stands apart from them, knowing what her MOTHER is going to ask her. Music stops.

FELIX: What happened to you, dear mother?

MOTHER: I was lucky. A German officer noticed my high German speech and took me as his own servant, and head cook for the labour camp. Working in the kitchen saved my life, and above all my sanity. I got to eat, if not my fill, then enough to stave off hunger.

FELIX: And Grandmother Esther?

MOTHER: Worked beside me. But she grew frail, and when typhus struck… Strange, how one goes on to the next task as if nothing has happened. I saw her die, but went on peeling the next potato or onion. I watched my mother's body swept away with all the others and did not cringe. A totally natural event. So unnatural I had become. *(MOTHER looks at YOUNG S.)* Now, Süssel, what happened to Father?

YOUNG S: Mother, you know I can't talk about it.

MOTHER: All the way from Czernowitz you didn't say a word about him.

YOUNG S: I know.

MOTHER: I'll wait as long as I can, but Süssel…

SÜSSEL & MOTHER: …some things have to be said.

MOTHER: Though they happened to you, they belong to Felix and me as well. Father's life was ours and so is his death.

YOUNG S: No, please don't, it's not necessary. Of course you both have to know. I'm sorry for hesitating so long. And, indeed, how would I have felt if you had not told your story? You know me, I'm selfish—perhaps I needed more time.

MOTHER: Yes, my child, I should know, shouldn't I?

> *MUSICIAN plays more of "In One Spot" during the following.*

YOUNG S: Well, then. I've told you both we find shelter with a saintly Ukrainian babushka, after we flee the camp. She keeps us for several days, lets us wash, eat, sleep, and restore ourselves. She tells us where the villages are, and gives us more than she can spare, I'm sure, to take with us on the road. The day is clear when Father and I leave, and we trek two, three days, in the direction she has pointed out. But no houses appear, and on the third day the weather changes.

> *Sound of growing winter wind. FATHER appears in the background, walking slowly, pushing into the wind. Heavy snow falls. SUSSEL joins him.*

The sky gets heavier, dark grey, and it snows constantly. We're covered in it, but still plough on, through heavier and heavier snow. The wind grows to a blizzard, so the whirls of snow obscure not just the horizon but the next step. It's futile. The snow perfectly roots us, so heavy it is, clinging to our Russian boots.

By early evening the temperature has fallen sharply; night is approaching. Father stumbles against something, perhaps a heap of boulders or a clump of stunted bushes. Beside it is a rather comfortable dip in the ground, and we settle alongside each other, as we always do, for nearness and for each other's animal warmth.

FATHER stumbles, then settles down with SÜSSEL in the snow.

YOUNG S: We don't even think of taking anything from the rucksack the old lady has replenished, we're so exhausted and wet with snow.

FATHER: Where do you think we are? Near the river?

YOUNG S: We look around, at a bluish-white expanse and a leaden-grey horizon.

SÜSSEL: All the directions look alike.

YOUNG S: So we settle in the snow.

SÜSSEL and FATHER huddle together.

When I wake, it's day. Bitter cold, the same sky as the day before. Father lies utterly still. His Russian hat has fallen off.

SÜSSEL touches his cheek. MUSICIAN plays "Kaddisch" melody.

There are no tears, no theatrics. I sit by him. Take a few things from him I think I can use, his pocket knife, the watch and chain Dr. Bauer returned to him the day before releasing us.

As YOUNG S speaks the following, SÜSSEL murmurs the beginning of the Kaddish.

SÜSSEL: Magnified and sanctified is God's great name throughout the whole World of Creation. May God's sovereignty by accepted in our lives and the lives of the People Israel and all peoples, soon and in our days, and let us say: "Amen."

YOUNG S: I say the beginning of the Kaddish, which I heard as a child; I'd forgotten the rest. Then I get up and start walking. Just guessing which way to go.

Lights down on FATHER. SÜSSEL makes her way

        back to her bed. Piano bell tone to finish "Kaddisch" excerpt, coordinating with snow scene vanishing.

        So that is the story. Not very heroic, I'm afraid.

MOTHER: I thank you for it, Süssel. And we are who we are, no matter what.

FELIX: Yes, and no object, no thing, matters.

MOTHER: But love matters. *(Beat.)* Dear Felix, here is the thing I owe to you. An almost incredible story. Ludmilla Bunin—

FELIX: Ludmilla! You've seen Ludmilla?

MOTHER: She came through the vastness of Russia to find you. We stayed a few days together, and she talked of her love. How it has changed her. It was perhaps one of the most beautiful encounters of my life.

FELIX: I loved her too. She saved us all.

MOTHER: She told me. Some things…

YOUNG S: I know you're right.

YOUNG S & SÜSSEL: Some things have to be said.

SÜSSEL: And there's more.

        MUSICIAN plays "Unter Di Churves Fun Polyn" ("Under the Ruins of Poland"), a Jewish folk song, as:

Scene Twenty-Nine: Mother

        FELIX and YOUNG S take MOTHER by a hand each and help her into bed, propped up on pillows. YOUNG S and FELIX sit on suitcases at her bedside. MOTHER is dying. Music ends.

YOUNG S:	Some applesauce?
MOTHER:	No.
FELIX:	A glass of milk?
MOTHER:	No. The purple pouch. Take it from under my pillow.

YOUNG S takes velvet pouch out from under pillow.

Please open it. *(YOUNG S does.)* Süssel, take my diamond earrings with the beeswax pattern. I loved them. They're from grandmother Esther. My wedding ring too, of course. Father's watch and chain, that Süssel took from father's waistcoat, is yours, Felix, as is this small medallion. And yes, there is something for Marusja. These few rings and golden chains. Children, please get them to her for me.

…It is time.

FELIX:	Mother.
YOUNG S & SÜSSEL:	Mother. Dear Mother.

She quietly dies. Lights down on the family. Music stops. FATHER enters and wheels bed around, then both exit.

MUSICIAN plays "Liebesleid" by Fritz Kreisler, a slow, gentle and reflective version, under the following:

Scene Thirty: Young S and Felix

FELIX and YOUNG S move downstage and stand, suitcases in hand, talking.

FELIX:	What will you do now, Süssel?

YOUNG S: A colleague from Prague has asked me to join a Czech resistance army unit as a pharmacist-chemist.

FELIX: You studied in Prague, so you speak Czech, don't you?

YOUNG S: Yes, and you can't.

FELIX: No, so I couldn't go with you.

YOUNG S: Where will you go?

FELIX: I'll stay here until the war is over. Then I think I'll go to Vienna.

YOUNG S: Where you studied.

FELIX: Yes. I loved Vienna once. Perhaps I will again.

YOUNG S: Let's spend as much time together as we can before I leave.

FELIX: Of course. It's too bad we have to part so soon: such is war.

YOUNG S: But the war is nearing its end, isn't it?

FELIX: I think so. There is hope. *(Music swells, brightly.)*

FELIX and YOUNG S exit. Music ends.

MUSICIAN: So you go to Prague.

SÜSSEL: Yes. And that…that is how I miss finding Max.

MUSICIAN: Finding Max where?

SÜSSEL: He's come to Bucharest too.

MUSICIAN: But you don't run into him.

SÜSSEL: No. Through chance, through fate. Who knows? Sometimes things just happen. Everyone is on the move.

More "Liebesleid" until scene changes.

Scene Thirty-One: Max, Helen, and Grisha

> *People are lined up at a passport office. A WOMAN gives the ROMANIAN POLICEMAN a thick wad of money and gets a passport. She leaves hurriedly. MAX is next in line. Someone nudges him forward. HELEN is nearby.*

POLICE: We're closing.

MAX: But my passport application is all complete.

POLICE: I don't care. We're closing.

MAX: Here, let me give you something. *(Fumbles in pocket for money.)*

POLICE: What's the name again?

MAX: Birnbaum. Max Birnbaum.

POLICE *(Takes it and decides it isn't enough.)* Are you trying to bribe me?

MAX: No, of course not. I'd never bribe a Romanian officer.

POLICE: Good. This isn't enough to be a bribe. *(Pockets it anyway.)* Come back tomorrow.

MAX: You said that yesterday!

POLICE: Tomorrow. *(Leaves.)*

> *Crowd leaves. HELEN comes over to MAX.*

HELEN: Please, I couldn't help hearing. Are you Max Birnbaum from Czernowitz?

MAX: Yes, I am.

HELEN: I'm Helen Meyer.

MAX: Helen Meyer? Did you say Helen Meyer?

HELEN: I did.

MAX: Of course, you're Helen. My Joey's Helen. *(He goes to hug her, but pulls back.)* Oh. Excuse me. You do know he died?

HELEN: I know. Others who escaped from the camp told me that. And about your friendship with Joey.

MAX: I see. He was a true brother to me. And he told me everything about you. You're just as beautiful as he said.

> HELEN *makes the gesture* JOEY *described, "and with her hands she'll fix a strand of her hair self-consciously, over her ears."*

HELEN: And he told you everything about me?

MAX: Yes. *(Embarrassed.)* Everything.

HELEN: Everything? Oh, dear. *(She laughs.)* Tell me what he said.

MAX: *(Pause.)* One day at the labour camp, dried fish arrived, and potatoes, rotten but still edible. We ate our fill. Later, under my warm Russian coat, memories of love came flooding in. He talked of you late into the night, though the five-o'clock roll call was pitiless. He told me about you expecting a child and his strong premonition that he would never see you again, or the child. "She is too beautiful," he said, "too vulnerable to face it all alone." "Joey," I said, "sleep now, or you won't be strong enough to stand on your feet at roll call. They'll shoot you if you can't work." And I whispered close to his ear, "I will find Helen and look after her if you cannot. Sleep now, my brother." I've been looking for you everywhere I go.

HELEN: Well, now you've found me.

MAX:	Really, you found me. But a strange sixth sense made me speak those words to Joey, that I would look after you—I who can't even tie my own shoelaces or cut a slice of bread. But it gave him ease and he fell asleep pressed against my shoulders.
HELEN:	I see. So are you ready to keep your promise?
MAX:	Of course.
HELEN:	To look after me, to take his place.
MAX:	To take his place?
HELEN:	I have a passport in his name. Tickets to Haifa. His daughter—
MAX:	His daughter!
HELEN:	Elizabeth. Do you have a passport?
MAX:	I...no.
HELEN:	Then you could take Joey's place by taking his name. Do you want to?
MAX:	Of course. Of course.
HELEN:	Then, since you already know everything about me, we'd better get married tomorrow.... Joey.

She embraces and kisses him. At first unsure, MAX quickly kisses her passionately in return. They exit.

Scene Thirty-Two: Prague again

MUSICIAN:	So they go to the Holy Land.
SÜSSEL:	They do. To live on the border of Jordan and what is to become Israel. It's 1947.
MUSICIAN:	And you're back in Prague.

SÜSSEL: Yes.

MUSICIAN: Are you happy?

SÜSSEL: I'm happy. But Prague has changed remarkably. All my Jewish friends, students, their parents, have perished in Theresienstadt, and I walk on the shores of the Moldava, that golden river, and do not sing as I did before. The air is poisoned.

MUSICIAN: But it's not all tragic.

SÜSSEL: Oh no. I find Czech colleagues, non-Jews, who offer me a partnership in their father's pharmaceutical plant.

MUSICIAN: Of course, the Russians must have taken a hold of the country.

SÜSSEL: The true economy flourishes underground. And I'm tired, tired of all the lies, the state having a hand in everything, and the constant inspection. Of course, we cheated.

MUSICIAN: Of course you cheated.

SÜSSEL: And so we are hugely successful. Anyway, I must get on with Max and Helen.

Scene Thirty-Three: Max and Helen

As SÜSSEL writes again, MUSICIAN plays Israel's national anthem, "Hatikva." MAX outside at night, looking up. The sky is filled with stars. Music morphs into starry sky music, underscoring the following.

MAX: So here I am, wondering what does it take to break the mould, leave the trodden paths to find truth with a piece of paper and a pencil in hand; looking through a ground-glass lens into the universe at a starry sky? What does it take to think one's own thoughts? To drive a wedge in the thousand-year-old assumption that we are the centre of it all? Geocentrism, the idea that the universe turns around us, everything lives to serve us. What does it take, to stand alone against powers that have Paradise for sale and Hell if you do not buy? What kind of man does it take? How mysterious, how cunning, and how exultant a man to go and find another to share a truth so dangerous to the dominant church and state! The wonderful letter Johannes Keppler wrote to Galileo about the findings of Copernicus—oh! I smile at the thought. Heavens, a German, an Italian, and a Pole thinking that the world is one, as in my father's faith, God is One. I like my father's Jewish faith. A credo with a number at the centre: One. With all the abstract thought to follow. Who can define a number? A tongue that speaks through itself, like music, so beautiful.

HELEN has come on during the above.

HELEN: Look at the stars. They're so brilliant. And you can talk to me about this sky—a different sky, just a little shifted from home. *(Caressing MAX.)* If you want me, we'll go behind the barracks. Come. I long for it—look, I'm wearing just this light shift-dress. It's days now—you say tomorrow and tomorrow—come my Joey, my Max.

MAX: We are stellar stuff, made of all that's out there. I ask myself, are we all made of energy, transformable into matter, and vice versa? If we are, then God is truly one, in all forms. *(Beat.)* Helen...

HELEN: Yes?

MAX: I have to go on a journey. Into the desert.

HELEN: Why?

MAX: A promise I made. Because of love. Long ago.

SÜSSEL: You don't have to keep that promise. You don't have to go.

HELEN: A promise. If you have to. But first... (*She starts to kiss him.*)

MAX: It'll be all right. Grisha will be with you.

She leads him off. Music ends.

Scene Thirty-Four: Grisha

MUSICIAN: Stop. Who is Grisha?

SÜSSEL: You weren't paying attention. Remember the camp, the escape across the river.

MUSICIAN: Ah, that Grisha.

SÜSSEL: I understand your confusion. On a journey like this, you meet so many people.

MUSICIAN: That's true.

SÜSSEL: So, Grisha. A young Russian Jew, only nine years old. His people had been herded into a ditch and shot during the advance of the Einsatzgruppen. Bullets were not wasted on children, and Grisha waited for the right moment, crawled out from under his dead mother and father, and ran. Later picked up by the SS, he was put to work in Max and Joey's camp.

MUSICIAN: So by the time he finds Max again in Israel, he is—

SÜSSEL: A young man.

MUSICIAN: And he moves in with them.

SÜSSEL: Yes.

MUSICIAN: Max, Helen, Elizabeth, and Grisha. A family made by the war.

SÜSSEL: If I'd only have known…

MUSICIAN: Known what?

SÜSSEL: I was so idealistic, so foolish.

MUSICIAN: In other words, you were young.

SÜSSEL: I should never have asked Max to go into the desert. Believe me, I didn't want it to turn out the way it did.

Scene Thirty-Five: Dead Sea caves

On one side of the stage, MAX is in a desert landscape. On the other side, HELEN lies ill in bed, with GRISHA attending her. MUSICIAN plays "Two Bagatelles" (op. 48, 1, 3) by Elizabeth Lutyens, improvising under the scene.

MAX: Why do I come here? To the desert slopes, to the Dead Sea caves. Here, with a killing sun above. It is not our Cecina sun, heavy, golden, benign, just hinting at its power. Here it shows its intent. Its finality. I am here to find your truth, Süssel, to go to your dry, exhausted lands, along the red rocks, the pale ivory rocks with their hollows, to seek. I am here for your truth, Süssel, not mine. My truth is simple. It grows out of a seed, an idea only, to be proven correct or false. This is my truth. It stands on its own. It is about the universe and our place in it, as a conscious part of the whole. It has a beauty of God-like splendour. So different from your truth, Süssel. Yours is intuitive, from the gut, an inner certainty.

GRISHA feels HELEN's forehead. He gives her water to drink. She's delirious.

HELEN: (*Calls out.*) My Joey! My Max! Joey! Where are you?

GRISHA: It's me. Grisha. I'm here, Helen. I'm here.

MAX finds a cave entrance, and moves inside.

MAX: I move from cave to cave, with the blinding sun in between. Find a flat dark hollow. Climb into it as into a mother's womb. It embraces me with the comfort of a heartbeat, a living pulse, a restful half-darkness. As if I have come home.

HELEN: Don't leave me! Come back! Come back!

MAX: The voice now speaks in letters. I see them in the half-darkness. Not on parchment. Signs and sounds overlapping. Thought clearing also. Almost linking into my own enchained truth. To find it One. Like yours and my father's.

I come not knowing what I'll find. I don't think I'll discover a scroll. What I find is a wonderful calm at the lowest point on earth, on the shores of the Dead Sea. Murder, rebellion, and hatred leave me. And inside, where man has hidden God's word, I have this moment all to myself, a moment of beauty, of partaking of the eternal.

MAX finds a shard of pottery, picks it up, and examines it.

What's this? A shard of ancient pottery. Perhaps it held a scroll at one time.

He puts it in his pocket. GRISHA holds HELEN's hand while she dies. He weeps.

HELEN: *(Murmurs.)* Oh, Max. Oh…

Music stops. Lights down on HELEN and GRISHA.

Scene Thirty-Six: Truly rootless

SÜSSEL: I didn't know she'd die while he was away. I didn't know. She got one of those tropical diseases that we from the north have no defences for. It was Shabbat in Jerusalem, when all work stops, no buses run. Grisha couldn't find a doctor until it was too late. Max went to the desert because of me, and Helen died in Grisha's arms.

MUSICIAN: You couldn't know.

> *MUSICIAN plays "Kaddisch." MAX is back home in the bedroom. HELEN's body is gone. Music ends.*

MAX: Oh, Helen. Helen. I went to the desert because of my promise to an old love. I left you here. And now you're gone. Now I'm afraid. Afraid of the emotions that make men here fall down and kiss the holy ground or stand at the foot of the wailing wall and shake in trance. I am not any more just a silly coward, as my brother said. But fear assails me, fear of the sacrifice asked. You have been taken.

SÜSSEL
& MAX: What further price will be demanded?

SÜSSEL: What does it cost to build a house of glory? To find His markings, His engraved letters, His thought, which is the real house of God. What will it cost?

MAX: Master Manole had it easy. He had command, the will and madness for sacrifice. I am not he. I am terrified of that price. I will not give precious life; it isn't mine to give. It has to be wrenched from me. Master Manole's altar is not mine. I look into the word of God to build that house for him. But what will it cost? The walls have crumbled, my Lutheran mother lies on the ground, so do my father and his people.

	So, beloved, what price ought to be paid for our wanting to be or not to be, our wanting to find purpose, or that supreme beauty that makes our being here so utterly worthwhile?
SÜSSEL & MAX:	Why payment? Why sacrifice? Why Master Manole, everywhere?
MAX:	No answer, sweetheart. We can only observe, as we do in the sciences, that this is so. All my walls have crumbled, they lie around me in heaps of dust.
SÜSSEL & MAX:	And there is no stone left in Jerusalem, where there is nothing but stone. There is no stone left to raise.
MAX:	I would have to be Manole himself to fashion the stone to finish the last chapel. I will not offer a life. Helen has been taken and I can't build a house. Not to God, not to thought or beauty. Not my house, for the wish to think, the wish to know, are gone.
	Oh, Helen. Oh, Süssel. This is how homeless we are. Existential creatures, having to know why they live, all the time. Formulating questions, asking God for answers. Pressing Him, who hasn't spoken since Job. And this querying is also our true homelessness. We are truly rootless. So I'll pick up the staff, my wedding band, our memories of youth, town, in heart, and wander.

MAX exits.

Scene Thirty-Seven: To Canada

SÜSSEL:	Poor Max. Poor Max.
MUSICIAN:	But he stays in Jerusalem, taking care of Elizabeth and Grisha.
SÜSSEL:	Yes.

MUSICIAN: And where are you?

SÜSSEL: Where am I? Leaving Prague.

MUSICIAN: When did you leave? And why?

SÜSSEL: After about five years, I'm restless. I get along very well with my workers and partners. But I'm somehow unable to forge any closer personal relationship. To fall in love, hold someone close, take him into my arms—or even just walk hand in hand along the Moldava. I'm too wounded, too guilty perhaps.

MUSICIAN: Where do you go?

SÜSSEL: I'm one of the few lucky ones. I get a Canadian immigration visa, open up a big map of Canada and let my index finger fall where it might. And it lands in the middle west on a spot with a wild name that I have never heard before nor know how to pronounce.

MUSICIAN: So you're happy to leave.

SÜSSEL: I don't anticipate the heartache I feel at leaving the golden city. My soul has adopted it and sung its tunes, but its soil is poisoned, as all European soil is, drenched in pain and loss.

MUSICIAN: So you have to go.

SÜSSEL: Yes, before I become old.

> *MUSICIAN plays "Un Canadien Errant" (Canadian folk song) to underscore:*

MUSICIAN: And how was the journey?

SÜSSEL: Everyone on the boat is a novel. Old and young with the future in their faces, going to Canada. In my life I've seen men and women emerging from despair, but I have never before seen hope working miracles. Going to Canada. Dreamland.

MUSICIAN: You're transformed.

SÜSSEL: For the moment, I'm free.

> Music ends.

MUSICIAN: But you don't know where Max is.

SÜSSEL: I try to find him through the Red Cross, suggesting Israel as a possibility, without success. Of course, he's taken Joey's name. My brother, Felix, is still in Vienna, where he's a pharmacist. And through him, I get in touch with Marusja.

MUSICIAN: Why do you need to find Marusja?

SÜSSEL: To send her something, and to make her an offer.

> MUSICIAN plays the music for "In a Sentimental Mood," words and music by Duke Ellington, Irving Mills and Manny Kurt.

Scene Thirty-Eight: Süssel's letter to Marusja

> MARUSJA opens a small package, taking out a letter, and a couple of rings and gold chains. As she does so, YOUNG S begins to speak.

YOUNG S: I always loved you, Marusja, and so did my mother. Your name was on her lips moments before she died. So dear you were to her. Here is something she wished you to have in her memory.

> MARUSJA puts on the rings and fastens the gold chains around her neck.

Marusja, come, come to us. There is room for you and Canada will welcome you. There are Ukrainian churches and people to talk to in your mother tongue. Come. But if you decide to stay in our homeland, I will send you the money to buy the piece of land adjoining your own, so you will have enough to live on. Let me know!

Forgive me, Marusja, but everything comes home to me now. Where we live the air is clear and bubbles like fermented wine.

Music morphs into a gentle underscore, based on "Blue Sky" from "Star Light, Star Bright," by Alexina Louie. SÜSSEL, YOUNG S and MARUSJA (reading the letter) overlap lines in the following speech.

YOUNG S: Cranberry Flats is a place of longing. No matter how much I love the open sky, the way the river seems to flow out of it, it is a place of longing. There is memory everywhere, no matter where you turn. Every newcomer feels it.

SÜSSEL &
YOUNG S: I talk to them—newly arrived, used to cramped European quarters, they are bewildered.

SÜSSEL: But we pilgrims learn to see. My friends, who come from all quarters of the world will ask one day: "Don't you think, Süssel, this river here, looks like my Danube?" "No," I will say, "not like the Danube…

SÜSSEL &
MARUSJA: …it looks like the Prut." And so it goes, with we immigrants.

SÜSSEL: We see what we know, what gives us comfort, what makes us feel at home. The air here gives you a light head, carries berries and blooms at the same time, the one coming, the other going.

ALL: A fragrance and a memory.

MARUSJA: All is back, your musty cellar, the difference between us, the love and the bond. In a place with a strange and lovely name—Saskatoon, Sas-ketch-e-van. *(Amused.)*

SÜSSEL &
YOUNG S: A place to live, the way you are, with all the baggage you carry.

YOUNG S: You know now where we are. Write, so we know how life is.

ALL: Write. We're here for you.

SÜSSEL &
YOUNG S: Love, Süssel.

Sequé volta to "Estrellita" by M. A. Ponce.

Scene Thirty-Nine: Süssel's letter to Max

YOUNG S clutches a letter from MAX.

YOUNG S: Oh, Max! Max! My brother Felix has found you for me. I am holding his letter with your Jerusalem address in my hand. My eyes are blinded with tears. That you are alive! And in Jerusalem!

Music ends.

MUSICIAN: Somehow you find him.

SÜSSEL: In the spring of 1951.

MUSICIAN: So…after Helen died.

SÜSSEL: And he takes back his real name. Birnbaum, Max Birnbaum.

YOUNG S: Dearest Max, my little brother-fiancé.

MUSICIAN: So you find him because…because she dies.

YOUNG S: The last time I saw your beautiful, haunted face was behind the barbed wire of the ghetto.

MUSICIAN: So you could have gone on living without him?

SÜSSEL: Of course. Of course. But, dearest Max, the only

fiancé I ever had!

Lights up on MAX reading the letter on the other side of the stage.

MAX: Dearest and sweetest friend, this will be a long letter, I'm afraid, to cover over ten years—but I must not go into small things, which I should leave for the day of our reunion.

YOUNG S: But let me give you an outline, at least, of my trajectory…

MAX rapidly scans the pages.

MAX: Bucharest! She was in Bucharest. At the same time as me?

YOUNG S: I work here in Canada as a pharmacist. And I have bought a piece of land. On the river, the spot of my dreams.

MAX: Belovèd Max…ah, she says "belovèd"…I've built a house.

YOUNG S: Dearest Max, did you ever kiss me? I fear you didn't and so I dare now to hug and kiss you. I still see your beautiful face behind the barbed wire…

MAX: …and I know you haven't forgotten me. My only belovèd, my once-fiancé.

SÜSSEL & YOUNG S
& MAX: Your Süssel.

Scene Forty: Max and Grisha

MUSICIAN: Of course, you invite him to come see you.

SÜSSEL: Of course. With the children, Elizabeth and Grisha. However…

MUSICIAN plays "Hatikva," which morphs into

star music, then an icy version of the anthem, dark, dissonant, ominous at times. MAX on the roof at night, looking up at the stars. GRISHA enters.

GRISHA: I want to be an astronomer. Like you, Max. But I'll go into the army first.

MAX: Army? We're leaving on the fifteenth of June.

GRISHA: Let's not go. I like it here now. I'll go into the army. Just three years and I can study in between.

MAX: Army? You want to wear a rifle with a bayonet on top? Guns were outlawed in my father's house. Do you want to kill?

GRISHA: Max, for heaven's sake. In the army, I'm armed. I can defend myself. Never again will we permit ourselves to be slaughtered. Besides, I spoke to a girl who's in the army. A little older than I am. I will marry her. Max, she's beautiful. Dark. Yemenite. Hair cut short, the limbs of a gazelle. Her name is Shoshanah.

MAX: So this is what it is, you're in love, Grisha, I promise you, when you have learned a profession and you're a young man, you can marry whomever you wish. But for the moment I make the decisions.

GRISHA: But we've been promised a shikkun—an apartment with electricity and an indoor toilet, within six months. Where are we going, Max?

MAX: To the fifty-second degree of latitude north, and we sail from Haifa.

GRISHA: What is the town called? You haven't answered my question.

MAX: It's hard to pronounce. It is called—after a fruit, a berry.

GRISHA: A berry? What do you mean?

MAX: A berry, round like the planet earth or a water drop. In fact, it's a member of the apple family.

GRISHA: Max, you're not serious.

MAX: I am serious. The city lies on a great river. It is one of the longest river systems in North America, and it flows into northern waters.

GRISHA: Northern waters? Who wants northern waters? I like it here. There is no winter. I've had, as you know very well, Max, every part of my body frozen. I'm not going there.

MAX: Grishinka, don't be so hard on me!

GRISHA: Max, look, you have a job here as a map-maker. This is a country for Jews. The future is open for me and Elizabeth. Sure, I'll have to be in the army. But my beautiful friend told me how much fun they have. Night fires in the hills, songs. The love of the country which is ours.

MAX: It's all true. I love my job, but I've made a decision for the first time! And not just for sentimental reasons. Let us try the new world. Grishinka, ancient as this land is, there is war, all around us. Israel has to prove itself. It will arm itself and fight. It is small, there is no land, not enough people to defend it.

GRISHA: We'll defend it.

MAX: Let me explain. Be patient with me. I'm your elder. Hard times are coming. Grisha, I can't face it again. There was slaughter in the tents just when we arrived. The country is surrounded now, it will certainly fight. I can see the fervour rising, the feeling of national pride, the determination to never again be murdered unarmed in your beds, or, what is worse, to be dishonoured, have your good name dragged through the mud. It's a young man's old land, I can see that, Grisha.

"Hatikva" in a cold but straighter version.

GRISHA: So it is just right for me, Max. I'm the young defender of whom you speak.

MAX: But it is I this time who makes the decision. You need a profession, a trade, you have to learn things. If that dark, beautiful face will haunt you, you'll be back for her. Trust me, I know. If it's yours, there is no escape. Not from young love. I've been there. Grisha, I know, if it is, it will be. You won't escape.

Music ends. MAX and GRISHA exit.

MUSICIAN: You know, you're getting good at this.

SÜSSEL: Good at what?

MUSICIAN: Creating the truth. This story telling.

SÜSSEL: Yes, I'm learning. Anyway, they all come to Saskatoon. Max, Grisha and Elizabeth. But that first meeting, I really see only Max.

Scene Forty-One: Süssel and Max

Music of "Blue Sky." Bright prairie light up as elements of the house appear. MAX arrives, suitcase in hand. He looks up at the house, then at the view, overlooking the river.

YOUNG S enters. He doesn't see her. She stands for a moment watching him. Her hair is "red-streaked silver, piled high in a chignon, like her mother's."

YOUNG S: So, you have come.

MAX: *(He turns to her.)* Süssel.

YOUNG S: I knew you would.

SÜSSEL & YOUNG S: No escape from early love!

SÜSSEL: It directs your footsteps, like fate.

MAX: No escape for you.

YOUNG S: Nor anyone.

> *They stand, looking at each other.*

MAX: This house is so like your grandfather's old house. Three stories high, with the river below. *(Looks around.)* And such a wide-open land.

YOUNG S: *(Laughs.)* There's nowhere for you to hide.

MAX: And, dear Süssel, you've found a spot where the river curls and bends that echoes our childhood's river valley. There is where we went to swim, and this is what we saw from the southwestern slopes of the Cecina. The river flows straight out of the sky, carrying the blue with it. Turns and twists to make its way through the sands, which hold the river, gilding its edges. A dream and a return.

YOUNG S: Come with me, down to the river.

MAX: The children—

YOUNG S: Can wait until we return. Come.

> *She takes his hand and they walk to a spot looking out over the river (the audience).*

YOUNG S: Look at the river.

MAX: The river valley wider than our valley, the bushes lower, aspen and poplar more gnarled and wind-tossed.

YOUNG S: I love to walk here in the late afternoon. The prairie stillness has an intensity and a beauty that exalts my heart.

MAX: On this high August day, the air remembers. Rose-fruit scented, orange-tinged, heavy with the past.

YOUNG S: All activity subsides, melts into that pure stillness.

> MAX takes from his pocket a pale ochre shard. He takes her left hand, puts the shard into it, and closes her fingers over it.

MAX: I picked up this when resting in one of the Dead Sea caves you sent me to, Süssel. Here it is. This pale ochre shard of stone. This is my wedding ring. It's yours now.

SÜSSEL &
YOUNG S: And the wedding day?

MAX: Tomorrow? Or as soon as the law of the land permits. Will you take my children as yours?

YOUNG S: If they want me.

MAX: How to speak of my love. A verse in Genesis says it like no other: "Jacob kissed Rachel and broke into tears."

> They kiss for the first time.

SÜSSEL: We travelled so far to find this moment, this first kiss.

> YOUNG S and MAX exit.

Scene Forty-Two: Marusja's gift

MUSICIAN: So you begin your time together with Grisha and Elizabeth.

> As scene changes, chaotic music, improvised on Stravinsky's "Piano-Rag-Music."

SÜSSEL: Yes, they're with us for five years. Doors banging, Elizabeth dropping her school books noisily, friends of Grisha with their guitars wanting to "crash" on the basement floor. Grisha graduates in mathematics and astronomy. Elizabeth is still in high school. But they return to Israel together.

Music ends.

MUSICIAN: And now you're truly alone with each other.

SÜSSEL: All things have their own time.

MUSICIAN: So that's the whole story.

SÜSSEL: Except…it's not quite the whole story. One day a package arrives.

> *MUSICIAN plays "Der Nussbaum." YOUNG S and MAX stand at an oval dining room table. They pry open a wooden crate and take out a note.*

YOUNG S: Here's a note from Marusja.

MAX: Not only to ease my conscience but to ease the conscience of the world. For penance and return.

> *MAX lifts a Rosenthal-white soup tureen out of wood shavings and places it at the centre of the table. MAX then takes out the ladle and sets it beside the tureen.*

YOUNG S: *(Astonished and pleased.)* Ah. The tureen. The only piece of my mother's porcelain I ever regretted losing. Its sheen is so beautiful. Marusja didn't have to do this. Thank you, Marusja, thank you.

SÜSSEL: The tureen moves along so perfect a curve. And yet it is an everyday thing that is set upon the one o'clock dinner table, carried by Marusja, or my mother herself. Containing something as simple and wholesome as potato-leek soup or chicken broth… Yes, I have longed for it, believed it irretrievable.

MUSICIAN: Yet here it is.

MAX pulls out the folded "Tree of Life" rug that has been protecting the tureen.

MAX: And what it this?

He opens it up to show YOUNG S the rug.

YOUNG S: The "Tree of Life" rug. It hung in our dining room.

MAX: It's beautiful.

YOUNG S: I'll put it over our bed.

YOUNG S takes the rug, as MAX exits, hangs it over the bed, puts on a bathrobe and lies down. Music ends.

Scene Forty-Three: So Desired

SÜSSEL stands near the MUSICIAN.

SÜSSEL: I think I'm nearly finished.

MUSICIAN: Do you need to rest first?

SÜSSEL: No. There's just one more thing for now.

MUSICIAN: What is it?

SÜSSEL: This.

YOUNG S in bed, sleeping. Nightmare music based on fragmented "Träumerei."

YOUNG S: *(Cries out in her sleep.)* No! No! No!

Music ends. MAX hurries in from his own bedroom, shirt undone, in sock feet, with book in hand.

MAX: Süssel? Süssel? Are you all right?

YOUNG S: What? Max? I...I was having a nightmare.

MAX;   I thought so. I heard you from my room.

YOUNG S: You were awake?

MAX: I'm not sleeping well either. Things seem to haunt me. My dreams...they weren't good. When I got up everything started spinning. I had to steady myself...

YOUNG S: It seems the past isn't easy to leave behind.

MAX: Should I make us some tea?

YOUNG S: No. Max, come here.

MAX: What?

YOUNG S: Do you know that twenty-five years have passed since I came to the ghetto with Dr. Bauer's letter in hand?

MAX: Is it? Almost to the day?

YOUNG S: Yes, and so much... *(Beat.)* Max, you're moving into my room. In the morning I'll help you carry your things. But now...will you hold me?

MAX: Of course. *(He climbs into bed with her, holds her and strokes her hair.)* Dearest Süssel. My love. So desired.

YOUNG S: Thank you, Max. Thank you. And I will always hold you when you need it.

             They lie together, holding each other tightly.

SUSSEL: And that's where I'm going to end my story.

MUSICIAN: You've done very well.

SUSSEL: I've left so much out. Perhaps I'll add it later. But now I think I deserve a little rest. A little peace.

MUSICIAN: Are those you remembered still asking anything from you?

SÜSSEL: I don't think so. I've helped them say what they needed to say.

MUSICIAN: Yes, you did.

SÜSSEL: Max kept telling me to write the story down and have done with it. Dear Max. It seems he was right. I wish I'd done this when he was still alive.

MUSICIAN: You've put things to rest then.

SÜSSEL: For me. *(Holds up notebook.)* But I've let all of them loose upon the world. It's strange.

MUSICIAN: What's strange?

SÜSSEL: They're all gone...yet they're all here. I wonder, could you play something in their memory?

MUSICIAN: Of course.

> MUSICIAN plays a tango-lullaby version of "Lullaby for Piano, Clarinet, and Strings" by the group Kol Simcha. SÜSSEL slowly moves to its rhythm. Other characters enter, first her FATHER, then her MOTHER, FELIX, MARUSJA, LUDMILLA, and DR. BAUER. MAX and YOUNG S move to join them. Slowly they circle around SÜSSEL, moving closer to her.
>
> Lights down. Music stops.

The End.